D0841848

MELVILLE PRISON AND DEADMAN'S ISLAND

AMERICAN AND FRENCH PRISONERS OF WAR IN HALIFAX 1794-1816

BRIAN CUTHBERTSON

FORMAC PUBLISHING COMPANY LIMITED

Formac Publishing Company Limited recognizes the support of the Province of Nova Scotia through the Department of Tourism, Culture and Heritage. We acknowledge the financial support of the Government of Canada through the Book Publishing Industry Development Program (BPIDP) for our publishing activities. Formac Publishing Company Limited acknowledges the support of the Canada Council for the Arts for our publishing program.

Library and Archives Canada Cataloguing in Publication

Cuthbertson, Brian, 1936-
        Melville Prison and Deadman's Island: American and French prisoners of war in Halifax 1794-1816 / Brian Cuthbertson.

ISBN 978-0-88780-837-1

        1. Melville Island Prison (N.S.)—History.   2. Prisoners of war—Nova Scotia—Halifax—History. 3. Prisoners of war—United States.   4. Nova Scotia—History—1784-1867.   5. Melville Island (Halifax, N.S.)—History.   6. Deadman's Island (Halifax, N.S.)—History.   I. Title.

FC2346.52.C88 2009   365'.971622   C2009-902374-1

Formac Publishing Company Limited   First published in the U.S. in 2010
5502 Atlantic Street   Distributed in the U.S. by Casemate
Halifax, Nova Scotia   2114 Darby Road, 2nd Floor
B3H 1G4   Havertown, PA 19083
www.formac.ca

Printed and bound in China

CONTENTS

INTRODUCTION

At a service on 30 May 2005 (Memorial Day in the United States) a commemorative ceremony was held on Deadman's Island in Halifax's Northwest Arm for the unveiling of a memorial inscribed with the names of 195 Americans who died while prisoners of war in Halifax, of whom 188 were buried on the Island. More than 10,000 French, Spanish and American naval seamen, privateers and soldiers, captured during the Napoleonic Wars and the War of 1812 with the United States, were imprisoned on nearby Melville Island. Of these, 270 are believed to have been buried in unmarked graves on Deadman's Island, which was then called Target Island.

French prisoners were first accommodated on Kavanagh's Island — officially renamed Melville Island in 1805 — in the 1790s, but it was the purchase of the island and construction of a prison building in 1805 that turned Melville Island into a military prison. It thus became part of a system of war prisons established by Britain to deal with more than 70,000 prisoners of war taken during the Napoleonic Wars and the War of 1812.

Although international conventions for the treatment of prisoners of war date back to the Hague conferences of 1899 and 1907, only since the Second World War has there been much scholarly interest in the subject. The Canadian historian Denis Smith discovered, while researching his *The Prisoners of Cabrera: Napoleon's Forgotten Soldiers 1809–1814*, that the fate of prisoners during the Peninsular War in Portugal and Spain had been only "glancingly treated." This is equally true for the War of 1812, for which there is a vast literature on other aspects of the conflict. A recent bibliography of the War of 1812, compiled by John C. Fredriksen, with hundreds of entries, lists just ten under the heading of prisoners. Of these, only one, an unpublished PhD thesis by Anthony Deitz, completed in 1964, could be described as a full-length study, and it considers only prisoners of war in the United States. Most prisoners' personal narratives listed by Deitz are related to Dartmoor Prison in England, but three — by Benjamin Palmer, Benjamin Waterhouse and Ned Myers — relate to experiences on Melville Island. For the French prisoners of war there is the diary of François Bourneuf, edited by J. Alphonse Deveau.

Histories of the War of 1812 and its various campaigns mention numbers of prisoners taken, but rarely tell us much about their fate. In *The Incredible War of 1812*, J. Mackay Hitsman has a single index reference to prisoners, relating to a possible armistice and exchange of prisoners early in the war. George Stanley's *The War of 1812: Land Operations*, published in 1983, has no index entry for prisoners at all. A history published in 1989 from the American perspective by Donald R. Hickey, *The War of 1812: A Forgotten Conflict*, does have a brief section on prisoners,

In 2000, the Halifax Regional Municipality turned Deadman's Island into a public park because of its historic significance.

mostly concentrating on retaliatory actions by both sides.

Of more relevance is a recent doctoral thesis (2006) by Paul Joseph Springer entitled *American Prisoner of War Policy and Practice from the Revolutionary War to the War on Terror*. It devotes a full chapter to the War of 1812, albeit entirely from the American perspective, and nearly all the documentation is drawn from American government sources. Springer notes, despite the large numbers of prisoners taken relative to the size of the of the forces engaged, that "most works discussing the War of 1812 see the POW problem as a minor issue, if it is discussed at all." He comments that while standards of treatment have evolved in wars involving American forces up to the War on Terror, "many decisions regarding treatment of captured enemies were made over two hundred years ago and the underlying principles of POW treatment remain unaltered."

In this book I have concentrated on Melville Island as a war prison from the perspective of the prisoners and their relations with Lieutenant William Miller, the British naval officer in charge of the prison, and John Mitchell, the resident American agent for his country's prisoners of war from October 1813 to December 1814.

There have been numerous articles on Melville Island, but the research has been limited to relatively few sources with the result that they tend to be repetitive. An exception, and the most comprehensive and most recent history, is *Deadman's: Melville Island and its Burial Ground* by Iris Shea and Heather Watts. For my history I have had the benefit of the sources used by past researchers, but also sources that have not been examined before — in particular the papers of John Mitchell. Most of his papers are held by the Library of Congress in Washington, but the Pennsylvania Historical Society also has a small collection. I am indebted to Kim Stevens for arranging to have the papers microfilmed and to the Nova Scotia Archives and Records Management, where the reels have been deposited, for contributing to the cost of microfilming.

Another major source has been American newspapers published during the War of 1812. These papers relied greatly on information from Halifax regarding captured privateers, the sailings of prisoner cartels and commercial and naval ship movements. They are often headlined "Latest from Halifax" or "Late from Halifax." When copies of Halifax's *Acadian Recorder* arrived they would note the fact. All the newspapers had columns on "Marine News" in which there would almost always be entries relating to Halifax. The New England and New York papers proved the most useful. I am grateful to Shannon Risk for undertaking research in Maine newspapers. I am much obliged to Henry Roper for reading the manuscript and for his editing expertise. This is my sixth book with Formac Publishing and as always I am grateful for the efforts by the editing, production and layout staff.

CHAPTER 1

ESTABLISHING MELVILLE ISLAND PRISON

Kavanagh's Island Fishing Station

On his map of the South Part of Nova Scotia and its Fishing Banks, printed by order of Parliament in January 1750, London map publisher Thomas Jefferys showed the Sandwich River on the northwestern side of the Halifax peninsula. Not only was this body of water not a river, but the original Haligonians also soon took to calling it the Northwest Arm. Jefferys' title and inset showing the fishing banks off Nova Scotia emphasized the commercial importance of the fishery to the fledging settlement, just six months after Edward Cornwallis and the first settlers had arrived and begun the arduous task of creating a town out of the wilderness.

For decades New England fishermen had been coming to the banks, but with the settlement of Halifax the inshore fishery could be exploited year round. Among the first of the settlers to see the potential of the Northwest Arm, which is well protected from Atlantic storms, for prosecuting the inshore fishery were Robert Cowie and John Aubony. Soon after their arrival they erected first a commodious storehouse and later a blockhouse with a stone chimney and two fireplaces on a small island on the west side of the Northwest Arm for which they obtained a Crown grant in 1752 that included the island and 160 acres of mainland.[1] The island soon gained the name Cowie's Island. On Cowie's death in 1781,

John Butler Kelly purchased the island, together with 500 acres, at public auction.[2] However, Kelly almost immediately sold the island and accompanying acreage to James Kavanagh.[3]

The Waterford Irish Kavanaghs were among the first English-speaking families to settle on Cape Breton Island, where they established a thriving fishing business at St. Peter's on the narrow isthmus separating the Bras d'Or lakes from the Atlantic Ocean. By the early 1780s, James Kavanagh was head of the family, and he decided to move to Halifax, where he planned to concentrate the family's fishing business. As was common with the naming

Soldiers of the Royal Nova Scotia Regiment guarded prisoners sent to Kavanagh's Island.

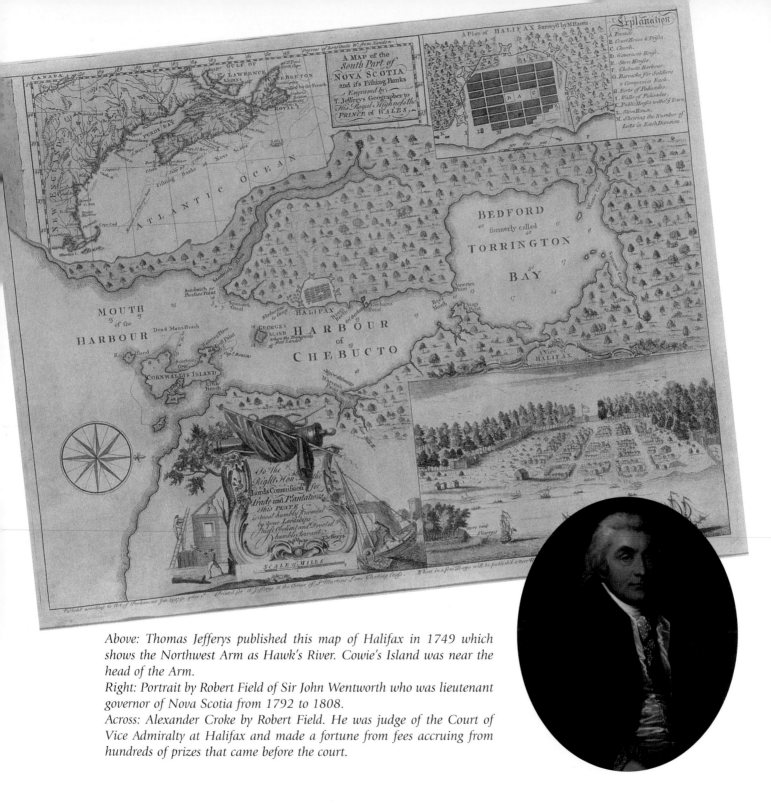

Above: Thomas Jefferys published this map of Halifax in 1749 which shows the Northwest Arm as Hawk's River. Cowie's Island was near the head of the Arm.

Right: Portrait by Robert Field of Sir John Wentworth who was lieutenant governor of Nova Scotia from 1792 to 1808.

Across: Alexander Croke by Robert Field. He was judge of the Court of Vice Admiralty at Halifax and made a fortune from fees accruing from hundreds of prizes that came before the court.

of islands, on Kavanagh's purchase of the island it soon became known as Kavanagh's Island. Kavanagh dried and stored fish on the island, and also operated an extensive business on the Halifax waterfront, exporting dried and pickled fish and importing salt, molasses and rum.

War with Revolutionary France and French Prisoners of War

News of the dramatic public beheading by guillotine of Louis XVI on 21 January 1793 reached Halifax in early April. Both citizens and the military garrison knew that this event made war between Great Britain and Revolutionary France inevitable. A week later news arrived that France had indeed declared war. Governor John Wentworth received orders to raise a provincial regiment, to be called the Royal Nova Scotia Regiment.[4] However, relations between the garrison commander, Brigadier General James Ogilvie, and Wentworth immediately became strained after a number of recruits to the Royal Nova Scotia Regiment proved to be deserters from Ogilvie's 4th Regiment. Ogilvie seized these men and returned them to the 4th, but they again deserted at the first opportunity. He refused to accept any responsibility for the new regiment, and obstinately ignored Wentworth's pleas for barrack space, clothing and provisions.

As soon as he could arrange the shipping, Ogilvie sailed off with two regiments to capture St. Pierre and Miquelon in the Gulf of St. Lawrence off Newfoundland. The French readily surrendered on 14 May and Ogilvie made arrangements for the 600 prisoners to be sent to Halifax. In preparation for the prisoners' arrival Wentworth sought a suitable site for their confinement, but without informing Ogilvie, he went ahead and rented Kavanagh's Island.[5] Of course, there would be contracts to be dispensed to his merchant friends for the feeding and care of the prisoners and his friend Kavanagh would

receive a handsome rent. Wentworth believed he could justify the rent and other expenses to the Secretary of State for War and the Colonies because on Kavanagh's Island the prisoners could be kept healthy and out of reach of all communication with Halifax.

When Ogilvie returned to Halifax in late June with the prisoners, he declared he would have nothing to do with Wentworth's scheme. He put the prisoners into the Cornwallis Barracks near Citadel Hill, appointed James Clarke as commissary of the prisoners and fed them from garrison rations. However, in December, several of the prisoners escaped from the barracks and fled into the countryside. Clarke posted notices in the *Royal Gazette and Nova Scotia Advertiser* offering compensation to those assisting in their capture, but it seems that they were never caught.[6] This incident no doubt gave added impetus to the removal of the prisoners from Halifax, and in June 1794 they were shipped off to Guernsey in the Channel Islands.

When a captured French vessel from St. Domingo was brought into Halifax in August with many of the French prisoners in desperate need of medical attention, Rear Admiral Robert Murray, commander in chief of the North American Station, accepted that more permanent arrangements would have to be made for dealing with prisoners of war. He first acted by appointing John Halliburton, chief surgeon at the Naval Hospital, as principal surgeon and agent for the care of sick and wounded naval prisoners of war.[7]

Above: By 1801 there were still only a few buildings on Kavanagh's Island. Troublesome French prisoners were kept in the ship's hulk, which can be seen at anchor on the far side of the island. Right: Charles Inglis, Bishop of Nova Scotia.

Halliburton also received authority to find suitable quarters for the wounded prisoners, which he succeeded in doing, only to face opposition from leading citizens who feared the prisoners carried a contagious fever. They protested to Wentworth. Halliburton explained to Wentworth that the surgeon of the vessel that had brought the captured ship into Halifax had determined that none of the prisoners had the fever.[8]

Such, however, was the fear among the inhabitants of Halifax that Wentworth and Halliburton agreed on the need for prisoners' quarters outside the town proper. Wentworth may well have suggested Kavanagh's Island because immediately after the meeting Halli-burton rode out to the island, which was two miles from town, where he found two empty houses.[9] Although the rents were exorbitant and the buildings in need of repair, he had no alternative. As he told Admiral Murray, if the wounded prisoners were quartered in the house originally selected in Halifax, then the populace would burn it down with the sick prisoners inside.

Murray still had to deal with the remaining prisoners. He searched the harbour for a vessel that could be purchased for use as a prison ship. *La Felix* was considered the best available and purchased for £250.[10] Next, he appointed James Lyman as commissary for the care of naval prisoners.

Lyman's instructions required him to pay particular attention to cleanliness and to providing correct prisoner returns. He could not allow officer prisoners to go ashore on parole without the express permission of Wentworth. If paroled officers went beyond their assigned limits or offended against the population, they were to be permanently confined on board the prison ship.[11]

By June 1795, 70 patients were held on Kavanagh's Island. Halliburton reported that the prison hospital was in constant use and he needed an additional surgeon.[12] Although Lyman's instructions were on no account to allow prisoners other than officers ashore, it seems that the increase in prisoners — there were more than 200 by mid-1795 — exceeded the capacity of La Felix, and some prisoners were allowed to live in the town. Another reason for allowing them ashore was the shortage of labour in wartime Halifax — French prisoners were much sought after as servants and for other occupations. Wentworth himself employed a prisoner, as did Bishop Charles Inglis and Judge Alexander Croke.

However, some of the prisoners living in town became so riotous that they were confined to Kavanagh's Island, probably in a 'hulk,' a decommissioned naval vessel moored offshore.[13] Soldiers of the Royal Nova Scotia Regiment were stationed on the island to guard them. Murray agreed that the Kavanagh Island establishment needed an assistant surgeon and that, because of its insular situation, a boat and crew had also become a necessity.

Murray, however, always hoped that the Kavanagh Island establishment would be temporary. In August 1795 he wrote to the British Consul General in Philadelphia requesting him to arrange with his French counterpart to send a vessel to Halifax to take away the French prisoners because it would "free us from the trouble of the Prisoners as much inconvenience will result from their remaining here during the winter."[14] But Murray confined 17 officers, who had broken their parole and tried unsuccessfully to escape by seizing a vessel, to the prison ship. They would not be part of any prisoner exchange because of "their breach of honour."[15] Nothing came of this attempt to be rid of the prisoners and the Kavanagh Island prison continued to operate.

Arrangements and Rules for Prisoners of War[16]

In making arrangements for handling prisoners of war at Halifax, Murray was following procedures well established by the Admiralty. After French prisoners of war started arriving in Britain, they were housed initially in a number of prisons erected during previous wars and then, as numbers increased, in prison hulks (by 1814 there would be approximately 70,000 prisoners of various nationalities). The Transport Board, an agency of the Admiralty charged with responsibility for prisoners, appointed agents — naval officers of the rank of lieutenant or captain — to be responsible for the administration of war prisons.

Turnkeys (literally keepers of the keys of a prison) as jailors had the most direct contact with the prisoners in the daily routine of prison life. A barrack master looked after the distribution of

Above: From Halifax's founding in 1749, the construction of fortifications remained a priority, especially for George's Island, depicted here, because of its importance for the defence of the town and dockyard. Right: Vice Admiral Sir Andrew Mitchell ordered the construction of Melville Island Prison building in 1805. Mitchell's heavy-handed attempts at impressment in Halifax earned him much enmity and were also an embarrassment for Attorney General Richard John Uniacke, his father in law.

bedding and clothing. An agent's clerk kept the various registers listing names of prisoners and details of their capture. Provision of rations was tendered every six months according to specifications laid down by the Transport Board governing their amount, type and quality. Prisoners were divided into messes and chose cooks from among themselves. There were no mess halls: prisoners ate in their barracks.

Agents had a set of rules, prepared by the Transport Board, that were to be observed by prisoners and the punishments that could be imposed for various offences. Punishments ranged from reduced rations to solitary confinement in a "black hole," a term dating back to the Black Hole of Calcutta — on the night of 20 June 1756, the ruler of Bengal had confined 146 Europeans in a prison space only 14 by 18 feet; by morning all but 23 of them had suffocated. Imprisonment in a black hole was the penalty for serious offences such as assaults on staff, violent assaults on other prisoners, attempts to escape and obdurate insubordination. Incorrigible prisoners were sent to the hulks. In the eighteenth century the prison system operated on the premise that there would be regular exchanges of prisoners between belligerents. A most effective form of punishment was to deny the prisoner his turn at exchange. This measure was used against individuals or groups of prisoners to ensure they obeyed the prison rules.

Strict obedience to orders was expected from prisoners, including answering to their correct names at musters. Fighting, quarrelling or inciting the least disturbance were strictly forbidden. And prisoners had to keep their barracks clean — any who refused to do so were deprived of their rations until they complied. Fatigue parties, consisting of one prisoner from each mess of twelve selected in regular rotation, undertook the duties of sweeping, washing, scraping and disinfecting their quarters. In the morning each man had to double his hammock over so that both ends hung on one hook, leaving the floor space clear. Prisoners were to appoint three or five of their number as a committee for examining the quality of provisions supplied by the contractor. Also, the committee had the responsibilty for seeing that they received full rations as to weight and measure that conformed to the victualling standards laid down in regulations. If not, the committee was to bring the matter to the attention of an agent and if necessary to the Transport Board.

During the eighteenth century procedures for granting parole to officers had been given formal status.[17] Its full term was *parole d'honneur*, as the word of honour of an officer was deemed to be of a specifically binding character. Parole could be granted for an officer to return to his native country upon entering into an engagement not to serve against Great Britain. Most paroles, however, were granted for officers to reside near a war prison and to receive a small living allowance provided by the British government. Breach of parole was judged a major military crime, punished by confinement in a prison hulk where offenders were treated as common soldiers or seamen. This was how Admiral Murray had dealt with the 17 French officers who broke parole in a failed escape attempt.

Murray's wish to be rid of prisoners of war was granted with the signing of the Treaty of Amiens in March 1801 between France and Britain. King George III described the treaty as an "experiment in peace," and disagreement over its clauses began immediately, but it did result in the return of all prisoners of war to their home countries. As soon as shipping was available, those in Halifax were sent to France. The Admiralty informed John Beckwith, its agent at Halifax, that he was to sell at public auction all remaining stores used by prisoners of war. It told Beckwith that it would not honour any outstanding bills after 31 January 1803. This would provide Beckwith with ample time "for abolishing the Establishment."[18] Four months later war broke out again and would last until the final defeat of Napoleon at the Battle of Waterloo on 18 June 1815.

Construction of a Prison Building on Melville Island

Almost immediately as war broke out some French prisoners were brought into Halifax. In the General Entry Book for French Prisoners of War, the first entry was dated 9 July 1803.[19] Vice Admiral Sir Andrew Mitchell approached Wentworth to accept these prisoners, but Wentworth insisted that they were the navy's responsibility. Mitchell, having no secure place for their reception, sent them to England. Some prisoners, however, while they awaited transport, were sent to Kavanagh's Island because on 23 August 1803, a detachment of one sergeant, five corporals and nine privates was ordered to march to the island to serve as a guard over French prisoners.[20] Mitchell also made arrangements to lease Kavanagh's Island and its buildings for one year at a cost of £100.

Meanwhile, the Admiralty had concluded that a full prisoner-of-war establishment was necessary at Halifax. It appointed Captain Robert Murray of the Royal Navy as agent at a salary of £400 with the authority, on his arrival at Halifax, to employ a clerk, an interpreter and a turnkey.[21] Murray arrived in Halifax in December to take up his appointment. The Transport Board had told Murray it had informed Admiral Mitchell that if no vessel could be appropriated for a prison ship at Halifax, then Kavanagh's Island could be purchased, if it could be acquired on reasonable terms. In May 1804, James Kavanagh put his island and its buildings up for auction.

Either at the auction, planned for 12 June, or beforehand, Murray purchased Kavanagh's

Island, its buildings and the surrounding 180-acre tract for £1000.[22] For this sizeable sum (Kavanagh had paid £65 for the property in 1784) the Admiralty obtained two buildings that had been fitted out to contain 200 prisoners, cookhouses adjacent to the buildings, a dwelling house, a barrack house for soldiers, a guardhouse and a boatman's house. On its purchase Kavanagh's Island was renamed Melville Island in honour of Henry Dundas, Viscount Melville, who had become First Lord of the Admiralty in 1804. The purchase of Kavanagh's Island was Murray's last duty as agent as he was promoted to rear admiral. His replacement was Captain John MacKellar.

Shortly after MacKellar arrived in late 1804, he submitted proposals for buildings and alterations at Melville Island. The numbers of prisoners of war being brought to Halifax had so increased that MacKellar requested the employment of a second turnkey, to which the Transport Board agreed, on condition that whenever the prison population dropped to 200, the second turnkey was to be immediately discharged.[23] This increase in numbers and the continuing concern for having proper accommodation during the winter months caused Admiral Mitchell to order the construction of a prison building on Melville Island in the spring of 1805.[24] MacKellar placed a tender call in the *Nova-Scotia Royal Gazette* of 11 April. It called for a wooden building 150 feet in length and 30 feet in breadth, one storey in height, but with two floors. It was to be built according to a plan held in MacKellar's Office. Although the Transport Board approved construction, with the proviso that its cost was not to exceed £1795,[25] by the time this authority arrived in September the building had been constructed and accepting prisoners since the early summer.

The plan referred to in the call for tenders was in all probability the work of William Hughes, who had been foreman of shipwrights in the Naval Dockyard since 1793.[26] Around the time the decision was made to erect the prison building, Hughes succeeded to the office of master shipwright. He has been credited as the master builder primarily responsible for providing the working plans for structures erected by Prince Edward, fourth son of George III, during his years in Halifax. He was also appointed to the building committee for the construction of St. George's Church on Brunswick Street. A year before the decision to construct a prison building, Hughes had prepared a report on the use of various woods by Nova Scotia shipbuilders. The tender call in the *Royal Gazette* went into considerable detail on the types of timber to be used in construction of the prison building, which strongly suggests that Hughes drafted the tender call as well as the plan.

In Britain, stone had been used for the construction of prisons, but there was a recent precedent for constructing wooden prison buildings. By the mid-1790s new prison accommodation had become essential as existing prisons and prison hulks could no longer house the numbers of prisoners of war. Plans were drawn up in December 1797 for a prison complex consisting of 16 barracks, each to hold 500 prisoners, at Norman Cross, Peterborough in Cambridgeshire.[27] Because of the immediate need, the complex was built of wood by carpenters employed day and night, seven days a week. It was partially ready for occupation by the following March, though a decision was made to add an extra storey to each of the barracks to increase the prisoner accommodation.

Although there is no evidence that Hughes had a detailed knowledge of the plans for Norman Cross, some similarities suggest he might have been aware of it. For the interior of the Melville Island building (as for the Norman Cross barracks) the tender called for rows of stanchions (upright posts) placed 8 feet from the

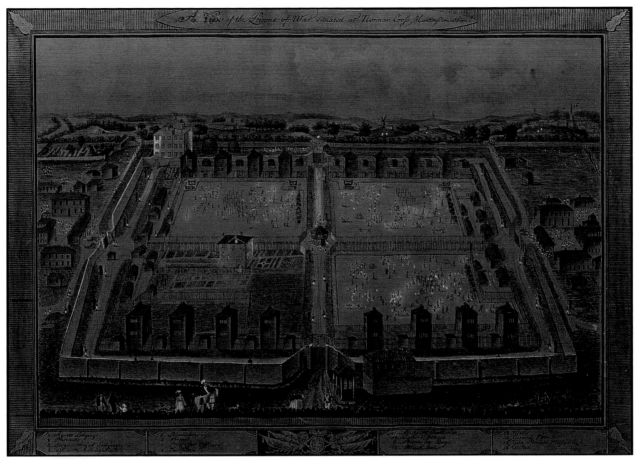

Above: By 1797 the need for another prison in Britain had become an imperative. It was therefore decided to build it of wood. The framework was constructed in London and conveyed to Norman Cross, Peterborough, where 500 carpenters and labourers were employed day and night, seven days a week.

inside walls on each side of the building, running down the centre and leaving a central corridor 14 feet wide. Half stanchions were built against each inside wooden wall opposite those in the centre. At night three tiers of hammocks were strung from iron cleats between each set of opposing stanchions. Every morning the hammocks were folded up and hung on the cleats on the walls on both long sides of the building, thus opening up the full space. Prisoners were probably allowed a lateral space of two feet for each hammock within the 150-foot-long barracks, which meant there would have been space for three tiers of 75 hammocks — room to accommodate 225 prisoners on each side for a possible total of 450 prisoners on the lower floor. On the upper floor, because of the steeply pitched roof, there were likely only one or two tiers of

Above: This photograph of 1929 of the prison's interior shows the stanchions upon which the prisoners slung their hammocks in three tiers. Right: French prisoners at Norman Cross, as at Melville Island, occupied their time by manufacturing bone and wood models of ships and anything else that caught their imagination and could be sold.

hammocks. In July 1805 the Admiralty ordered the construction of Dartmoor Prison in south-west England because of poor conditions on prison ships. It would have five long rectangular stone barracks, each capable of holding 1500 prisoners. Each had two floors and treble tiers of hammocks slung on cast iron pillars.

French Prisoners on Melville Island

Between 1803 and 1813 some 1,535 French prisoners would be held on Melville Island. After a short-lived peace, war was renewed when Napoleon returned from exile on the island of Elba; his final defeat came at Waterloo on 15 June 1815. During this period, more French prisoners arrived between February and August 1814. French prisoners were sent either to Melville Island, or placed on parole and required to reside across the harbour at Dartmouth and Preston. If they were sent to Melville Island the agent's clerk, with the assistance of an interpreter, recorded in an Entry Book not only the names of prisoners, but also details of capture, when received in custody, and whether the prisoners were exchanged, discharged, died or escaped. A copy of the records was sent to the Transport Board for administrative purposes and also for prisoner exchanges. Each prisoner was issued a hammock and a single blanket in summer and two blankets in winter. They were then divided into messes of seven and allocated their hammock space in the prison building.

As required by the regulations, MacKellar placed in the *Royal Gazette* calls for tenders for such items as bedding and "necessaries" like soap, and every six months for the supply of provisions — primarily beef, bread and salt. Initially, no contractor could be found to provide both beef and bread, so the Transport Board ordered that the two be separately tendered. The problem lay with the rising wartime demand in

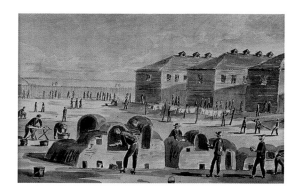

Halifax for fresh beef for crews of the Halifax squadron and the Naval Hospital. A contractor, Capel Hians, reputed to own most of the live-stock in the region of Halifax Harbour, held both these contracts, and in 1804 he also obtained the contract for Melville Island prison which he apparently would hold until his death in 1811.[28] When the Northwest Arm froze over in winter contractors had to carry the provisions and supplies around the head of the Arm. When the Arm was not frozen, they could bring the provisions to the shore on the Halifax side, from where the prison boat would transport them across to Melville Island.

The provision of clothing remained a contentious issue with the British government which maintained that it was the duty of each nation to provide clothing for those of its nationals who became prisoners. The French never accepted this responsibility for their prisoners held by the British, leaving the British prison authorities to supply clothing to those prisoners who were destitute of clothing. The British, however, had a further reason, other than humanitarian, to issue clothing, and that was to dress the prisoners in conspicuous colours, chiefly yellow, as an aid in detecting any who escaped.[29] Such apparel was called 'slop' clothing. At Melville Island the first issue of slop clothing took place in early 1806. A

Above: After a fierce engagement lasting six hours on 5 July 1809, HMS Bonne Citoyenne *captured the French armed transport* Furieuse *on which François Bourneuf was serving. Right: Among items made by French prisoners of war held by the Maritime Museum of the Atlantic in Halifax is this ship model, ca. 1810. Other items believed to have been made by French prisoners are privately owned.*

notice appeared in the *Royal Gazette* from the Office for Prisoners of War, warning all persons against purchasing the clothing, which was marked: "P. of W. signifying Prisoners of War, in red print, on the outside back of the Jackets, and black on the inside — On the thigh of the Trousers, and on the breast of the Shirts — and with the word Prisoner, on the inside of the shoes."[30]

For their messing arrangements, each prisoner received one half pound of meat per day, which was weighed by the butcher.[31] Each mess of seven prisoners had an 18-inch-long spit with a number. When the meat was cooked, the cook, who was paid for his skill and labour, took a large iron fork and put it into wooden tubs. Then he rang a bell, and each prisoner approached with his wooden bowl. Using a large copper ladle, the cook gave each a spoonful of broth and his ration of meat. Every second day the butchers and bakers on contract brought supplies of meat, bread, potatoes and salt. As provided in the regulations a prisoners' committee could report

poor quality to Captain MacKellar. There was a new tender call every six months, so contractors knew that they could lose contracts if the prisoners were dissatisfied.

While Britain and other European powers fighting France relied on recruitment and impressment to maintain their armies and navies, the French instituted a *levée en masse*. As a result, among the French prisoners held in the large prisons like Norman Cross in England and at Halifax, there were many skilled painters, jewellers, shoemakers, carpenters, fencing masters, music masters and other similar occupations. As a small boy, Halifax's noted historian Thomas Beamish Akins well remembered how many of the French prisoners were ingenious workers in wood and bone. Melville prison was "like a small town fair," especially on Sundays and holidays, when it was the favourite resort of the town's young people, and where a pleasant hour could be passed in conversation with the prisoners and examining the goods for sale.[32] Visitors could purchase snuffboxes, knives, forks, dominoes, hats, stockings, mittens and gloves.

Among themselves the prisoners held lotteries. They marked cards with the name of articles they had made and sold them to each other. Prizes could range from ivory toothpicks, or a box of dominoes to shaving brushes. The French prisoners were most remembered for their ship models, rigged with silk and cannons made from pennies. It took up to six months to make them. The scale of their operations can be gauged by their purchasing more than 1,000 ox bones a year from Halifax butchers and annually more than 4,000 pounds of wool. The most extensive collection of workmanship by French prisoners is held by the Norman Cross Gallery at Peterborough, England. Others put their talents to work brewing spruce beer, catching fish, making butter, and candy from molasses. Still others were allowed to work for wages in Halifax, but were not recorded as being on parole. Stonemasons, shoemakers, tailors and especially servants found ready work in Halifax and their services were in much demand.

Those confined on Melville Island were initially allowed to leave the island and wander about in the woods, but when some of them took the opportunity to escape they were confined to the prison. There were other breaches of discipline. When the prison garrison officers' fuel allotment was increased, but not that of the prisoners, the prisoners pelted the men bringing the officers' fuel and broke the windows of their quarters.[33] More serious was the fatal stabbing with an eating knife of a prisoner, Jean Marie Querrie (or Quenie) by a fellow prisoner, Pierre Poulin, in April 1805. Both were soldiers from the French frigate *La Ville de Milan*, captured by HMS *Leander* on 23 February 1805 and brought into Halifax as a prize. The guards had some difficulty in rescuing Poulin "from the rage of the others, who were present and saw the crime perpetuated," which was good reason to remove him from Melville Island and place him in the Halifax gaol.[34]

Although Captain MacKellar wanted a special commission to try Poulin for murder, lieutenant governor Sir John Wentworth refused. As he informed Vice Admiral Sir Andrew Mitchell, such a commission would supersede the established form for administrating justice in Nova Scotia.[35] Wentworth's refusal was probably influenced by the tense relations existing between himself (and his council) and Mitchell over Mitchell's high-handed attempts at impressment to crew his ships. The tension would lead to a deadly riot in Halifax in October in

A view of Melville Island by J.E. Woolford showing the signal system between the island and Fort George on top of Citadel Hill.

which one man was killed and others were severely injured.[36] Mitchell would have to pay heavy fines in civil court as a result of one of his press gangs breaking into a mercantile establishment. Although Wentworth did not mention that violent prisoner deaths in Britain were dealt with by the civil authority, he was no doubt relying on the advice of Chief Justice S.S. Blowers in refusing the Navy's wish for a special commission that would in all probability include naval officers.[37] Wentworth also gave as his opinion that it might furnish pretense to the French to inflict sudden cruelty on British prisoners.[38]

Poulin remained in the Halifax gaol until his trial before the Supreme Court on 12 July. An interpreter was provided for him, though the only witnesses called were two of the prisoners who had tried to murder Poulin before the prison guards had intervened. The jury of 12 found him guilty. After the trial Chief Justice Blowers prepared a report, in which he detailed its fairness and the jury's decision to find Poulin guilty of murder, for which the punishment was hanging.[39] Wentworth suspended the execution until he received instructions. These came from Lord Castlereagh in September, informing

Wentworth that the sentence could be carried out and that in future cases he was to use his own judgement.[40] Poulin was hanged on the Halifax Commons at the foot of Citadel Hill on 24 October, and he was buried in an unmarked grave.[41]

Much of what we know about life among the French prisoners of war comes from the autobiography of François Lambert Bourneuf, written from memory when he was an old man. After his schooling, his bourgeois family had sent him to sea to serve with his uncle, but around 1804 he was called up for compulsory service with the French navy. While serving on the frigate *Furieuse* in a battle with a British frigate in the mid-Atlantic, he was severely wounded. The battle lasted for some six hours before the *Furieuse* was forced to surrender on 6 July 1809. On arrival in Halifax Bourneuf was taken to the Naval Hospital, where he remained until he was well enough to be sent to Melville Island. Although in his autobiography he portrays an almost idyllic existence for French prisoners, he also mentions the existence of a prisoners' *Grande Conseil*, whose composition he does not describe, but which passed sentences on those prisoners who had committed punishable offences against their colleagues.[42] Bourneuf cites the example of a prisoner divulging his knowledge of a planned escape. He claims that the culprit was taken to a place well hidden from the English, bound and stoned to death by the whole company, according to the sentence imposed by the *Grande Conseil*.[43]

At Dartmoor, French prisoners elected from among themselves *Commissaires*, who were responsible to the prison governor for the maintenance of good order,[44] although the prison governor himself determined punishments, of which the severest was imprisonment in the *cachot* or black hole. At Melville Island Prison Bourneuf's *Grande Conseil* apparently served a similar purpose in maintaining discipline among the prisoners. However, the stoning of any who betrayed an escape attempt is improbable. Melville Island was a mere four acres in area and ringed by sentry posts, and it is difficult to see how a stoning could have escaped the notice of the sentries.

At least 130 French prisoners escaped either from parole or from Melville Island. Only eleven were recaptured, all except one after the War of 1812 had begun.[45] Those who were recaptured were put in the black hole, located in the cellar under the prison building. Prisoners in the black hole, with its iron bars and where daylight could only be seen through a small opening above the door, were fed only bread and water, though fellow prisoners were allowed to share part of their rations with them. Prisoners involved in fighting were also thrown into the black hole.

Notices of prisoner escapes appeared regularly in Halifax newspapers, offering rewards for their capture and giving such details as their facility in speaking English, how they were dressed, and where they were last seen or reported. As the years passed the notices changed from "ignorance of the English language" or "speaks a few words of English" to speaks "good English." Such was the case in the escape in 1809 of Pierre Frank who "speaks good English formerly lived as a servant to Sir John Wentworth last seen on the Windsor Road."[46] When captured in 1804 he had been serving as a seaman. He was never recaptured, perhaps finding a willing master of a merchant vessel to take him on as crew, who would have ignored the printed notices from the Office of Prisoners of War threatening prosecution for all masters of vessels "harbouring or assisting" prisoners to escape.[47]

As the war continued the labour shortage became acute, causing the Office of Prisoners to charge that escaped prisoners "have been seduced into the service of certain persons residing in the country" or that some persons "have enticed away and do actually harbour and conceal French Prisoners of War."[48] The largest escape took place on the night of 25 July 1805 when 14 prisoners kept in the Dartmouth Depot stole a ferryboat, presumably with the intention of seizing a coastal vessel and making for an American port. There is no record of their being recaptured.

Escapes and attempted escapes by French officers on parole residing at Dartmouth and Preston were taken very seriously. Twenty-five French officers were successful in escaping from 1803 to 1811. In 1807 a plot for a general escape of prisoners led by two officers on parole was discovered. The officers were sent to Melville Island and the prisoners' ringleaders were put in irons.[49] Prisoners on parole who engaged in what was considered disorderly conduct, and those who breached their parole conditions, were also sent to Melville Island, where they were treated as ordinary prisoners. Ever watchful for what it considered unnecessary expenditures, the Transport Board reprimanded MacKellar for the charges in his accounts for retaking prisoners, which were higher than allowed. In future he was not to pay more than one guinea.[50] MacKellar was likely paying out greater sums in a desperate attempt to increase recaptures.

The best-known successful escape from Melville Island was that of François Bourneuf in 1812.[51] Like other French prisoners, Bourneuf was allowed to work on the roads under overseers. Food was brought from the prison, and the prisoners slept in the overseers' houses. One night Bourneuf and some other prisoners stole a boat from Purcell's Cove on the Northwest Arm and sailed along the south shore of Nova Scotia hoping to find an American privateer. They were, however, captured and placed in the Shelburne town jail. Bourneuf then managed to escape from a vessel taking the prisoners back to Halifax

and made his way to Pubnico, near Yarmouth. There he taught school until Abbé Sigogne, a Roman Catholic priest who had excellent connections with officials in Halifax, arranged for Bourneuf to take the oath of allegiance. Another 63 French prisoners took the oath of allegiance, a good number of them while employed by Halifax inhabitants in various capacities.[52]

Melville Island Prison in 1812

A survey completed of Melville Island Prison grounds by John Toler, when complemented by contemporary watercolours, provides a reasonably accurate visual description of the buildings and layout in 1812. A bridge on the Island's north side connected it with the mainland and the road to Halifax, but supplies, garrison reliefs and visitors usually arrived by boat from the Halifax side of the Northwest Arm. On the Island's north side was the two-storey prison barracks, painted red, 130 feet in length and 30 feet wide. There was a one-acre prison yard or parade where the prisoners could exercise and where daily roll calls were held. Toler's survey shows officers' quarters. In 1808 this house required major repairs, so Vice Admiral Sir John Warren, who was now commander in chief of the North American Station, ordered it to be rebuilt, a decision for which he later received approval from the Transport Board. As agent, Captain John MacKellar advertised a tender on 29 July that called for the building of officer quarters to the specifications of a plan that could be seen at his office, to be completed by 1 November.[53] The foundation stone for the officers' quarters was laid on 1 September 1808,[54] and the rebuilt house was later incorporated into the Armdale Yacht Club clubhouse.

Other buildings included the turnkey's house, cookhouses and a barracks for the soldiers responsible for guarding the prisoners. An adjoining building housed the bell that

Above: This view of Melville Island taken in the 1880s shows the prison building and the officers' quarters. Background: John G. Toler of the Royal Engineers prepared this plan of Melville Island two months after the first American prisoners arrived upon the declaration war in June 1812. It graphically shows the number, types and the relationship of the various buildings on the island.

summoned the garrison or prisoners for roll calls. Around the island's perimeter were sentry boxes. A strong stone wall (150 feet in length, 8 feet high and 6 inches at the base), for which the Office for Prisoners of War issued a contract in September 1813, enclosed the prison barracks on the island side, facing the mainland, and on the other there were high wooden palisades.[55] It seems that in the spring of 1814 the construction of a "Barrier Wall" was also undertaken.[56] Also located in front of the officers' quarters were cannons sited to fire at the prison barracks. Communication with the Halifax Citadel and garrison headquarters was by means of a telegraph system using flags, and at night lanterns, which Prince Edward had established in the 1790s.

Of all the decisions that were made for turning Melville Island into a prison, none was to cause more difficulty than whether or not a separate building should be constructed to serve as a hospital. This would have been in addition to the Naval Hospital in Halifax, primarily for sick and wounded British seamen, and the Naval Prison Hospital at Dartmouth for prisoners of war — at an unknown date (possibly as early as 1794) a building at Dartmouth was used to house prisoners of war, which also served as a hospital for them.[57] In late 1806 MacKellar proposed to the Transport Board the erection of a hospital building on Melville Island and sent an estimate of the cost. The Transport Board informed Admiral Mitchell that the cost "amounts to so considerable a Sum, compared to the Advantage which can be expected to be derived from it," that it could not recommend to the Admiralty the incurring of such an expense.[58] It directed Mitchell to appropriate part of the present buildings on Melville Island for a sick berth, at least until some other arrangement should be found absolutely necessary. By July 1806 a "Berth for Sick Prisoners" had been established on Melville Island instead of a hospital, to the satisfaction of the Transport Board.[59]

There was also dissatisfaction with the costs, amounting to £600 a quarter, for victualling sick prisoners. When the Transport Board discovered that three French surgeons, who were on parole, were being victualled on the account for sick prisoners, it ordered the payments to cease and

The Warden's House in 1929, which during the War of 1812 had housed the officers of the garrison guarding the prisoners.

for MacKellar to report on the reasons they had been allowed to remain so long and at so very great charge. In June 1806, the Transport Board had ordered the closure of the Dartmouth hospital, located in a house with a boat crew, turnkey and steward employed there, because of the expense. However, on Dr. John Halliburton's representations the board had relented and approved its continuance, only months afterwards to order that "the whole of the very expensive Establishment at Dartmouth" be abolished.[60] Yet, it was still in being in August 1807, with the Transport Board objecting to sick prisoners from Melville Island being sent to Dartmouth in all seasons.

In August 1807 the board also wrote MacKellar that it could not understand the expense submitted by MacKellar for fitting up part of the Melville Island prison for a hospital. It told him that, "rather than keep Dartmouth, it would be better in every respect to build an additional room on Melville Island for a hospital."[61] In December the Transport Board would inform Admiral Sir John Warren, commander in chief of the Halifax Station, that it strongly approved the fitting up of the upper part of the prison building for the accommodation of the sick; it did not doubt that it would be "found to answer every purpose of a Prison Hospital."[62] This area would continue to serve as the prison hospital until Melville Island closed as a war prison.[63]

CHAPTER 2

PRIVATEERS, PRISONER EXCHANGES AND PRISON LIFE

Causes of the War of 1812

After the collapse of the short-lived Treaty of Amiens in 1803, the war against Napoleon Bonaparte became a life-or-death struggle for Britain. Anglo-French economic warfare intensified as Britain tightened regulations for neutral ships trading with France. As the United States had the world's second largest mercantile fleet after Britain and had the world's largest neutral merchant marine, it was especially affected. The Royal Navy began seizing increasing numbers of American merchant ships for contravening regulations. To make matter worse for the Americans, in 1806 Napoleon declared the whole of Britain blockaded; his decrees excluded from French-occupied harbours all neutral vessels that had entered a British port and declared all British-made goods lawful prize even when owned by neutrals. The French and their Spanish, Neapolitan and Dutch allies seized hundreds of American ships and their cargoes.

But what caused the most damage to American trading were the British Orders in Council that required all neutral shipping that wished to trade with French-occupied ports blockaded by the British to clear British customs first. In an attempt to force Britain to remove the Orders in Council, President Thomas Jefferson and the Republican-dominated Congress imposed an embargo on the export by American vessels of American goods. Not only did the embargo fail to change British policy, but it also devastated American maritime trading, especially that of New England. It is estimated to have cost the jobs of 55,000 seamen and perhaps 100,000 more in related industries.[1]

Britain retaliated by opening free ports in Nova Scotia and New Brunswick. An immense smuggling trade grew up, with American vessels bringing provisions and other goods into the free ports to exchange for British manufactured goods and West Indian rum and sugar. The British army under the Duke of Wellington fighting Napoleon's armies in Portugal depended on American provisions, so this clandestine trade was a strategic necessity.

Napoleon Bonaparte as he appeared in 1812 in a portrait by the well known French painter David.

Nothing, however, angered Americans more than the Royal Navy's cavalier policy of impressment, a result of the continuing shortage of seamen and a high rate of desertion. Estimates of the number of British seamen employed in the expanding American merchant marine and also in the fledging navy vary, but the figure was in the tens of thousands. Some of these were certainly deserters. The British took the position that once a British subject, always a subject. The number of American seamen pressed into the Royal Navy also remains unknown, but an estimated 10,000 seamen who had some claim to American citizenship were pressed between 1796 and 1812.[2]

Senior British naval officers encouraged high-handed actions in the desperate need for men, and none more than Vice Admiral Sir George Berkeley, commander-in-chief of the North American squadron, who issued orders to HMS *Leopard* to search for deserters who had signed on aboard American ships, in particular the USS *Chesapeake*. While at sea *Leopard* intercepted *Chesapeake* and when negotiations failed, she opened fire, causing the surprised *Chesapeake* to haul down her colours. After boarding, *Leopard*'s crew seized four seamen, claiming they were deserters.[3] In 1811 two of the seamen were returned to the United States. One of the others was convicted of desertion and was duly hanged from the yardarm in full sight of Halifax's waterfront, and the fourth man died in Halifax in the Naval Hospital.

Although the incident led to the removal of Berkeley, the Americans did not forget the gross affront to their national honour as Britain and the United States slid into a war. Despite the affront, many in the United States opposed the conflict, and the British most certainly did not want it while the struggle against Napoleon continued to absorb all its naval and military resources.

Historians have debated the causes of the War of 1812 at length. They readily fall into two groups: those who place the emphasis on maritime issues dividing Britain and the United States and those who argue that the root cause was American western expansionism.

Paradoxically, the most vocal support for war came from those on the western frontier who wanted to drive the British from the North American continent and who believed that the British were supporting Indian opposition to western settlement. Opposition to war came from the seaborne trading and mercantile interests, principally of New England. President Thomas Jefferson, despite assuring Americans that the conquest of Canada was "a mere matter of marching,"[4] was not in favour of war. But his successor as president in 1800, James Madison, owed his election to the "war hawks," who claimed that Upper and Lower Canada were there for the taking, and was more amenable to their calls for war.

Those who opposed war feared the Royal Navy, which was considered unchallengeable after the Battle of Trafalgar in 1805. At the time the American navy consisted of 16 warships and a few useless gunboats. A fierce opponent of war, John Randolph, a member of the House of Representatives for Virginia, declared that "... we hear only Canada, Canada, Canada ... It is agrarian cupidity, not maritime rights, that urges war. Not a syllable do we hear of Halifax."[5] A few days before the United States declared war, Federalist Senator Obadiah German of New York told Congress during a debate on augmenting the navy that, "Halifax and New Brunswick would remain unconquered without a maritime force to aid the land armies." He challenged those supporting the war to consider the country's maritime frontier, and judge what would be the consequences of war against the foremost naval power.[6] Such pleas, however, could not overcome the rising demands for war. Madison succumbed and signed the declaration of war on 18 June 1812. Ironically, just before the declaration the British government repealed the Orders in Council that ostensibly were a major reason for declaring war. The reasons given in the American declaration of war on 18 June 1812 were entirely maritime in nature — most especially impressment of American seamen and the Orders in Council that so curtailed American shipping.

Privateers and Prizes

At Halifax, Vice Admiral Herbert Sawyer, commander-in-chief of the North American squadron, did not learn of the declaration of war until 27 June, when HMS *Belvidera* sailed into port after nearly being captured by an American squadron. Three days earlier, off Nantucket, two 44-gun frigates of the American navy under the command of Commodore Rogers had attacked the 36-gun *Belvidera* without warning. She was fortunate to escape with only a few of her men killed and wounded. On her way to Halifax she captured three unarmed American vessels, the first of 711 prizes that would be brought into Halifax during the war.[7] In the hopes that the war would be short lived, Sawyer and Lieutenant-Governor Sir John Sherbrooke adopted a policy of deliberately not antagonizing New England, whose opposition to the war was well known. Sawyer issued instructions to his captains that they were not to molest any coasting or fishing vessels and not to commit any hostilities on the coasts of the United States. When, for example, Captain Benton of HMS *Spartan* captured the brig *Mary*, he gave her cap-

tain a certificate, certifying that he had liberated him and seven men as prisoners of war, while requesting him to use his endeavours to have the same number liberated if there were any English prisoners in Boston.[8]

Sherbrooke took advantage of the determination of the citizens of the District of Maine to "preserve a good understanding with the inhabitants of New Brunswick, and to discountenance all depredations on the property of each other." He issued a proclamation directing all the inhabitants of New Brunswick to abstain from "Molesting inhabitants living on the shores of United States, contiguous to this Province of New Brunswick and on no account to Molest the Goods, or unarmed Coasting Vessels belonging to the Defenceless Inhabitants...."[9]

The War of 1812 was to be the last major war in which privateering was accepted by all belligerents as a legally acceptable military activity. During the reign of Elizabeth I, more than two centuries earlier, merchant vessels could obtain letters of marque from the government that allowed them, while engaged in regular trading, to capture enemy vessels as the opportunity arose. The profits arising from the voyage usually came from the cargoes carried. Privately armed vessels that sought to capture enemy shipping — as prizes to be sold and the proceeds divided among owners and crews — were known as

Above: Thomas Jefferson by Charles Wilson Peale. Although he said the conquest of Canada would be "a mere matter of marching," Jefferson was not in favour of going to war with Britain.

privateers, a term coined by Sir Leoline Jenkins, a judge of the High Court of Admiralty (1668–85), as a means of differentiating them from pirates.[10] By the War of 1812, admiralty law, as far as Britain and the United States were concerned, had established what prizes were legitimate within the context of the law of nations.

Faced with the blockades and embargoes of two decades of Anglo-French warfare, American merchant ships were built for speed, with profits to be gained from low-bulk and high-value cargoes. Such vessels could be readily converted into privateers, and could outsail British naval vessels. They carried a mixed armament with one or more "long toms," usually carried amidships and designed to intimidate merchant ships. Other smaller calibre guns could be used if resistance was encountered. Privateers carried large crews, far in excess of the number required for sailing and fighting the ship. When prizes were captured, a small crew would be placed aboard under the command of a prize master and ordered to sail to the nearest home port. A good cruise could result in three, four or more prizes. Often, however, one or more would be recaptured.

Within days of declaring war, the United States Congress, with great enthusiasm, passed an act to encourage and to govern privateering. It covered such matters as the issuing of letters of marque and reprisal and provided the legal framework for privateering. The act met with much approval. In a letter to Paul Hamilton, the Secretary of Navy, the leading merchants of Salem wrote how, within ten days of the war's declaration, eight privateers carrying 400 men were at sea and another three ships carrying 16 to 20 guns and 100 to 200 men were nearly ready to set sail. Sixteen prizes had already been sent into Salem and more were expected. However, the merchants were concerned that many of the prisoners taken in these prizes were about to return to Halifax to be exchanged. They would carry with them a full knowledge of Salem's exposed situation. They requested the deployment of two gunboats as soon as possible to aid in the defence of the harbour and town.[11] Their request was not granted, but the British did not begin raiding operations on the New England coast until near the end of the war.

As soon as they received their commissions from the government, American privateers swarmed into the Bay of Fundy, around the Nova Scotian coast and into the Gulf of St. Lawrence. One, if not the first, in the Bay of Fundy was the sloop *Jefferson*, armed with one swivel gun

This poster depicts the British impressment of American seamen. It is estimated that as many as 10,000 American seamen were forced to serve in the Royal Navy between 1796 and 1812.

Portrait by Robert Field of Sir John Coape Sherbrooke, lieutenant governor of Nova Scotia, 1811-1816.

and under the command of George Crowninshield Jr. She arrived at Moose Island (technically an island, but in reality part of the American mainland) in Passamaquoddy Bay. George Crowninshield first went ashore, where he was informed by the Committee of Safety of a neutrality agreement between Maine and New Brunswick. Although he promised not to molest any persons, he immediately seized a schooner.[12] Other privateers followed and also ignored the neutrality agreement. The schooner, *Fame* of Salem, owned by the crew, sent two prizes into her home port in early July — an English ship of 300 tons loaded with spars and timber, and a brig of 200 tons loaded with naval stores, both from St. Andrews, New Brunswick bound for England.

The Crowninshields, the leading merchant family of Salem, owned the *Jefferson* and would own other ships, notably the *America*, with which their firm made great profits. They had extensive mercantile interests and intimate connections with the Republican Party. Over the opposition of many in Salem, the family had actively supported President Madison and the declaration of war. Benjamin Crowninshield, when running for the Massachusetts State Senate in October 1812, was accused of being personally interested in continuing the war and the question being asked was, "Is not the privateering system, in which he is so largely concerned, the surest pledge of his adhering to this destructive contest, even in opposition to the interests and wishes of his Constituents?"[13] Salem was bitterly divided over the war.

Although initially the privateers were able to cruise with impunity, the naval ships stationed at Halifax, led by HMS *Belvidera* and HMS *Spartan*, soon began capturing privateers and their prizes. The crews of

The Crowninshields were the most important mercantile family in Salem. Members of the family were among the first to engage in privateering on the declaration of war. The family had close connections with the Madison administration and greatly favoured the war.

the merchantmen taken by *Belvidera* — *Fortune*, *Pickering* and *Malcom* — became the first Americans to be sent to Melville Island Prison.

Meanwhile, in January 1812 Lieutenant William Miller, a Royal Naval officer, had replaced Mackellar as Agent for Prisoners of War at Halifax in January 1812. A veteran of campaigns in the Mediterranean and Portugal, Miller had obtained the appointment of agent for prisoners in Bermuda in 1803, through the interests of General Sir John Moore.[14] On 4 July 1812 he received the first American prisoners of war at Melville Island and opened a book, named the "General Entry Book of American Prisoners of War…." in which he listed not only the names of prisoners, but also details of their capture, when they were received into custody, and whether the prisoners were exchanged, discharged, died or

escaped.[15] For those taken at sea, the ship's name was recorded and later also for captured soldiers, their regiment and the battle in which they had been captured were listed. David Stickney, master of the merchant vessel *Fortune*, became the first American prisoner recorded in the Entry Book.

HMS *Spartan* captured the first privateer, the lightly armed *Active* of Salem, in the Bay of Fundy with a crew of 20 on 10 July. She proved not worth taking to Halifax as a prize and so was burnt. At the outbreak of war, Captain John Morgan took *Fair Trader* of Salem straight to the Bay of Fundy. She had a crew of 25 and a single gun. Almost immediately she captured an English ship of 400 tons, mounting two 6-pounders and with a crew of eighteen.[16] Morgan sailed *Fair Trader* under the stern of the ship and

Above: The more daring of American privateers cruised off the Sambro Light and the approaches to Halifax Harbour. Some such as Buckskin *out of Salem had success until her capture by HMS* Stratia. *HMS* Atalante *pictured here was successful in capturing American prizes until, while entering Halifax Harbour, she struck the dreaded Blind Sisters ledge off Sambro and sank; fortunately, all the crew managed to get ashore. Left: An American officer.*

fired the only gun she had. The crew of the ship, some of whom were Americans, left their guns and refused to fight, with the result that *Fair Trader's* crew boarded without any resistance. Four of the ship's crew immediately joined the *Fair Trader*. Continuing her cruise *Fair Trader* captured a small vessel carrying gin and tobacco. Morgan decided that the sale of the cargo and vessel would not pay the expenses of sending her to Salem so he gave her back to the owner. *Fair Trader's* luck ran out on 16 July when she could not out-sail the 18-gun brig of war *Indian* and was captured. *Indian* also had the good fortune to recapture an English barque taken earlier as a prize by *Dolphin* of Hallowell, Maine.

Buckskin, out of Salem with a crew of 34, captained by Issac Bray and mounting a single gun, chose to cruise off the Halifax's Sambro Light. During a fog *Buckskin* came across a large ship. However, the vessel had 24 gun ports, so Bray was fearful of making an attempt on her. Later, when he saw next day what he thought to be the same vessel, he changed his mind and determined to run her down with the intention of boarding. He did not discover his mistake until his ship was under the guns of the frigate *Stratia*.[17] Up to *Buckskin's* capture she had had earned good profits from her prizes, one of which she had apparently taken just outside Halifax Harbour.

Until the capture of the *Carlew* of Salem, captained by William Wyer of Salem, the privateers

In a fiercely fought action on 19 October 1812, lasting 45 minutes, the USS Wasp *defeated HMS* Frolic. *She, however, suffered such damage that she had to surrender to HMS* Poictiers, *which fortuitously appeared two hours later.*

had been small vessels like *Buckskin* with little armament. The *Carlew* was considered the equal, if not superior, to any privateer out of the United States.[18] She was a remarkably fast sailer, mounted 16 guns and carried a crew of 96. She had twice been chased by British frigates, which could not come up with her. But she had the ill fortune during a fog to run into the *Acasta*, a 44-gun frigate, which gave chase. After two and a half hours the *Carlew* struck her colours and was taken into Halifax, and on 27 July her officers and crew were marched through the city to Melville Island.[19] Shortly afterwards the *Acasta* captured the *Catherine* out of Boston, with 14 guns and a crew of 54. The engagement took place just outside Halifax Harbour. It lasted one and a half hours, and the boatswain and a first lieutenant were killed before the *Catherine* surrendered.

Under the headline "Bad News" the *New England Palladium* of 28 July 1812 described the capture of the 14-gun brig USS *Nautilus* and her crew of 89 under the command of Lieutenant William Crane after a seven-hour chase by HMS *Shannon*, captained by Philip Broke, during which the *Nautilus* threw overboard all her guns in the hopes of escaping the better-armed *Shannon*. However, she was taken because of "tempestuous weather." No guns were fired on either side. The *Palladium* reported that *Nautilus*'s officers were treated with much respect. Captain Crane's sword was returned to him by Captain Broke as an acknowledgement of the skill and bravery with which he had endeavoured to save his ship. The

Nautilus was the first American warship captured.

By the end of August, the Halifax squadron had captured 24 privateers, more than 40 merchant ships and the USS *Nautilus*. The number of prisoners taken — privateers, merchant seamen and United States Navy seamen — totalled more than 1500. American newspapers opposed to the war carried what were described as "Black Lists" of vessel losses. Pacificus in the *Boston Centinel* reported losses at 54 vessels, but this only included 13 privateers when the true total was 24.[20] The *Salem Gazette's* Black List since the start of "Madison's War" relied on reports from Halifax and had a total of 56 vessels.[21] The discrepancy between these totals and those of the official record kept at Halifax arises because some captures had not yet arrived at Halifax and also because the newspapers' information came from varying chance reports of Americans on parole or those arriving at American ports in cartels for prisoner exchanges.

Admiral Sawyer's policy was to be "very civil to American prisoners."[22] Maine's *Portland Gazette* reported that crews initially had been allowed to go about Halifax at large until Halifax citizens and authorities learned of "depredations of our privateers."[23] Prisoners were then confined to Melville Island where they were separated from the French and were reportedly well treated. From the arrival of the first prisoners, Sawyer approved returning them in neutral ships and placing them on parole in the United States. However, in August the number of prisoners had increased dramatically to 1,000, and Sawyer wrote to the Admiralty that he might have difficulty feeding them.[24] As a solution to accommodating that number, Sawyer arranged for the purchase of a captured

American sloop, the *Magnet*, for £2,474 and anchored her off Melville Island as a prison ship.

In the first months of the war most of the privateers were generally small vessels that were quickly converted for cruising. During the autumn of 1812 larger vessels appeared. Captain Joseph Weeks sailed the *Rapid*, mounting 16 guns and carrying 82 men, from Portland. He had considerable success, capturing a ship with a cargo valued at $250,000 and two brigs that he ransomed back to the owners. However, shortly afterwards *Rapid* fell in with two British frigates, and was captured after a chase lasting seven hours and during which Captain Weeks had thrown overboard all the guns, boats and every movable article in a vain effort to escape. Nonetheless, she had paid for herself many times over with prizes.

On her capture the Federalist *Columbian Centinel* commented that "the loss of this valuable vessel and the capture of a number of our worthy citizens, who from necessity rather than choice have resorted to privateering, is a consequence of this detestable war, and it is to the authors of it, that calamities and losses we experience by it is justifiably chargeable."[25] After adjudication by the Court of Vice Admiralty in Halifax, *Rapid* was commissioned as HMS *Nova Scotia*.

The *Thorn*, sailing out of Salem with a crew of 147 and mounting 18 guns, also had the good fortune to capture a rich prize, a ship of 300 tons sailing from Jamaica to London, before she herself was captured. By the end of 1812 a total of 2,078 prisoners had been recorded in the Entry Book. They consisted of 1412 privateers, 572 merchant seamen and 94 men from United States naval vessels. Beginning in July and August cartels with American prisoners, with the connotation marked in the Entry Book "On Parole," were dispatched mostly to Boston and Salem. During the autumn months the numbers of cartels increased and around 1,100 prisoners were sent not only to Boston and Salem, but also to Portsmouth and New York.

Still, there remained hundreds of prisoners and they were being held longer than in the early months of the war. During the autumn of 1812 items began appearing in American newspapers about poor rations and ill-treatment. The sailing master of the privateer *Lewis* out of New London, who had spent two months at Melville Island, complained his fare was "wretched indeed" and that he was "almost starved." When he complained, he was shown a "federal" paper printed in Boston (likely the *Boston Centinel*), stating that the "American prisoners at Halifax were very humanely treated and were furnished with wholesome provisions!!!"[26]

The master of the merchant vessel *Melantho*, out of Baltimore, who spent about two months on parole, claimed that American prisoners "were treated in a most shameful manner by the British agents."[27] The crews of captured vessels were landed under a strong guard, and conducted as if they were "criminals" through Halifax to Melville Island. He was much upset that the masters of merchant vessels were detained as prisoners of war, though on parole. Their parole permitted them to walk within the distance of only one mile of Halifax, but they could not go into any field or crossroad, nor be absent from

Left: An American artilleryman.
Right: An American rifleman.

their lodgings after 6 o'clock in the afternoon; nor quit their lodgings in the morning until the bell rings 6 o'clock. However, he said that he had been civilly treated while in Halifax. Another report from masters of the captured *Rapid* stated that while they had been treated very well on board HMS *Spartan*, on arrival at Melville Island, their trunks and baggage were searched and their quadrants, charts and spy-glasses taken from them by the turnkeys by order of William Miller. On the evening previous to their release they were told that "no priva-teerman's nautical instruments would be given up."[28]

War on the High Seas

During 1812 and 1813 the war on the high seas went badly for the Royal Navy — in single-ship actions the larger and better-gunned American frigates emerged victorious. They had larger crews, who were all volunteers and well trained. Many of the seamen in fact were British. Their commanders proved highly competent and brave leaders in battle. The first British loss came early in the war when the USS *Constitution* defeated HMS *Guerriere*. With twice the number of crewmen as *Guerriere*, *Constitution* was able to fire three broadsides to every two by her opponent. The desire to have *Guerriere's* surviving crew returned added impetus to prisoner exchanges, because the Americans now had British seamen to exchange.

In October, the sloop of war USS *Wasp* came across the remnant of a British convoy that had sailed from Honduras under escort by the brig HMS *Frolic*. They were fairly evenly matched, but *Wasp's* gunnery proved superior. The battle lasted 45 minutes. *Frolic* lost 17 dead and 45 seriously wounded; *Wasp* had only 5 killed and 5 wounded.

However, *Wasp* was so badly damaged that when the British warship *Poictiers* arrived, she had no choice but to surrender. The crew were first taken to Bermuda as prisoners. As was the practice the British examined all captured crews to determine if any were British subjects. Of the *Wasp's* crew, nine were deemed to be so and sent to Halifax.[29] The remainder of the crew were paroled and arrived in New York in late November.

Also in October the USS *United States* captured HMS *Macedonian*, which suffered grievous casualties in the action. After the battle the two crews got on famously, bearing out the belief that seamen of the day had more loyalty to their profession than to either their nationality or their ship.[30] Then, on 29

Left: A reproduction of an 18th century general-use sundial compass. Above: The battle on 1 June 1813 outside Boston Harbour between HMS Shannon *and USS* Chesapeake *was one of the bloodiest on record in the age of sail, though only 11 minutes separated the opening round until the* Chesapeake *surrendered.*

December, in what is considered the most tactically elaborate of three great American frigate victories, the USS *Constitution* defeated HMS *Java* off the Portuguese coast.

The Tide Begins to Turn

By early 1813, the British had sufficient warships to blockade much of the American navy in harbour. The Admiralty in London instructed the blockading force to draw the Americans into battle, where superiority of numbers would give them victory. This was not to happen, and the commercial war at sea continued. That year 36 privateer vessels were captured with 1,130 crewmen. During 1814 another 22 privateer vessels were captured and more than 1,000 men imprisoned at Melville Island. During 1813 and 1814 a total of 553 prizes, mostly merchant vessels, came before the Court of Vice Admiralty and more than 3,000 merchant seamen were sent to Melville Island.[31]

Among the privateers captured was *Thomas* out of Portsmouth. Before her capture she had earned great acclaim from New Englanders when, on 11 June 1813, she had taken *Liverpool Packet* out of Liverpool, Nova Scotia, commanded by Joseph Barss, Jr. *Liverpool Packet* was co-owned by Enos Collins, Benjamin Knaut and the brothers of Joseph Barss, John and James. She was formerly a slave ship — small, sleek and fast. It had taken the much larger *Thomas* five hours to close with *Liverpool Packet* and board her.[32] Several of the marines aboard *Thomas*, however, fired into the *Liverpool Packet* after she had been taken, killing three of their own crew, mistaking them for those of *Liverpool Packet*.[33] *Liverpool Packet's* first cruise had taken place in August 1812 and over the succeeding months she had earned a reputation as a scourge of American coastal trade. As *Liverpool Packet* approached the Portsmouth wharf with her captives, her prize crew fired a salute of 17 guns. There was much pleasure and satisfaction that this famous but insignificant-looking little ship was at last captured.[34] Such was the loathing for *Liverpool Packet* that her captain and crew were marched through the streets to the town gaol shackled in irons.

Joseph Barss was about to pay for the British ill-treatment of Captain William Nichols and his crew of *Decatur* that had taken place in January 1813.[35] After their capture the prisoners had been taken to Barbados, where the crew were confined to a dungeon under the town gaol and badly treated.[36] Initially, Captain Nichols was paroled, but he was recognized as having committed a crime before the war, and was also cast into the dungeon. When the American government discovered the treatment that had been meted out to Nichols, it retaliated by ordering the confinement of Joseph Barss and another British captain named Woodward. Their confinement and treatment proved to be "more than ordinary [sic] severe."[37] Lieutenant-Governor Sir John Sherbrooke was eventually able to have Barss, who agreed to forswear privateering, freed. Some Portsmouth merchants purchased the *Liverpool Packet* and renamed her *Portsmouth Packet*, but she was soon recaptured and reappeared as a prize in Halifax, where she was purchased by her former owners and again became a scourge to American coastal shipping. By the time she made her last cruise in the autumn of 1814, her privateering success had brought at least 60 and perhaps as many as 100 captures into Halifax.[38] Needless to say, her owners made fortunes, and none more than Enos Collins, who would become the wealthiest man in British North America.

Another case where a captured vessel was purchased and then sent to sea as a privateer to prey upon American shipping was that of the privateer *Thorn* out of Marblehead. A consortium of Maritime merchants, mainly from Liverpool, purchased her, renamed her *Sir John Sherbrooke* and sent her to sea as a privateer in March 1813. For a privateer she was heavily armed and able to carry a large crew. Some consider her to have been the finest privateer in the Maritime Provinces.[39] She mounted 18 guns and carried a crew of 150, including 50 sailors to act as marines. She had considerable success in bringing prizes into Halifax, but she was best known for her role in the saga of the American privateer *Young Teazer* out of New York and commanded by Captain William Dobson.

While cruising off Lunenburg in June *Sherbrooke* pursued *Young Teazer* into Mahone Bay. British warships joined in the attempt to capture her. The mate aboard *Young Teazer* was Frederick Johnson, a deserter from the Royal Navy. When he realized *Young Teazer* faced certain capture, he touched an open flame to her powder magazine. Of her 36 crew members, 28 were killed. For generations afterwards there were reputed sightings of *Teazer's* ghost and re-enactments of her fiery end.

Agreements for Exchanging Prisoners of War

In the eighteenth century, agreements between warring states for the treatment of prisoners became the normal practice. The agreements went beyond arrangements for prison exchanges and paroles. They included provisions for the treatment of prisoners and also set out the responsibilities of the prisoners' state of origin and where they were detained. Prisoner exchanges took place while fighting continued, conducted by agents who resided in their opponent's countries and by the use of cartels, ships with neutral status while transporting prisoners being exchanged.

During the first months of the War of 1812 there was no formal system in place for prisoner exchanges between Britain and the United States,

Inset: Joseph Barss of Liverpool, Nova Scotia and master of the Liverpool Packet.
Above: The Liverpool Packet, *Nova Scotia's most feared privateer and the scourge of New England shipping.*

but both sides had good reasons for adopting a liberal policy for exchanges because of the costs and resources needed to accommodate and feed prisoners. With the concurrence of Lieutenant-Governor Sherbrooke, Vice Admiral Herbert Sawyer permitted captured American merchant ship masters, chief mates and passengers to return to the United States on parole, on condition that they not take up arms against Great Britain until a regular exchange was worked out involving a similar class of British prisoners.[40] Sawyer, however, was emphatic that he had no intention of exchanging those taken as privateers, while there were any other prisoners.[41] He asked for instructions and received orders from the Admiralty that American privateers were to be considered the same as other prisoners.[42]

After the capture of the *Nautilus* in late July, Lieutenant William Crane had written to Paul Hamilton, Secretary of the Navy, to call his attention to the situation of American prisoners at Halifax. He had received assurances from Admiral Sawyer that prisoners from the *Nautilus* would receive every indulgence. Should they remain until the winter they would need clothing and many other "necessaries" to make them comfortable, which he had no funds to provide.[43] There were also in Halifax many hundreds of American prisoners taken from private armed and merchant vessels, who looked to their government for assistance. It had been suggested to Crane that a government-authorized agent for prisoners in Halifax, to attend to their exchange and wants, might greatly lessen their hardships. He had a conversation with Lieutenant William Miller, an officer of the Royal Navy, "a most excellent and humane gentleman," who strongly recommended a person should be appointed American agent. Miller told Crane that the British government could not furnish beds, bedding and clothes, except for the sick, though in fact prisoners received both hammocks and blankets.

Miller assured Crane that United States navy prisoners would be separated from the others and that their officers could visit them daily, inspect their clothing and cleanliness and furnish them with any comforts they may require. All Crane's letters sent and received by him had to be submitted for Miller's inspection; otherwise he would have written more openly to Hamilton.

The Americans had no organisation in place to deal with prisoners.[44] Moreover, there were no agreed-upon rules between Britain and the United States on how exchanges should be conducted. By August the Americans had secured the willingness of Admiral Sawyer "to enter into an arrangement for a general exchange of prisoners captured at sea."[45] Because of the large number of privateers and merchant seamen being captured and confined in Melville Island Prison, the appointment of a prisoner's agent at Halifax had become an administrative necessity for the American government.

It settled on John Mitchell of Philadelphia, the former consul at Santiago de Cuba, to be its agent at Halifax. Secretary of State James Monroe provided Mitchell with instructions for his appointment, the object of which was "to take charge of all American seamen, who are or may become prisoners at Halifax, and to send them home as soon as they are exchanged...."[46] Monroe emphasised that Mitchell was not to allow a large number of American prisoners to accumulate at Halifax. He was to provide for their subsistence and see that the sick were properly taken care of. Monroe made no direct mention of privateers or merchant seamen becoming prisoners. However, Mitchell was to assist any American citizens who were not in the land and naval service of the United States, but made prisoners at Halifax and were destitute.

Mitchell arrived in Halifax on 6 October 1812. He was highly pleased with his reception from ranking British naval officers.[47] His immediate task was to arrange for the return of the mounting numbers of American prisoners. Although he assured Washington that he would confine himself to non-controversial subjects in accordance with his instructions, he resolved that, "My Eyes and Ears shall be open. My Mouth only shall be shut."[48] When Lieutenant-Governor Sherbrooke reported Mitchell's arrival, he informed London he had reason to suspect that the new agent was also "Commissioned to communicate to His Government such information as he may from time to time be able to collect."[49]

Almost immediately on Mitchell's arrival, British authorities began pressing him to negotiate an explicit arrangement for the formal exchange of prisoners based on an agreed "tariff" of different values according to rank. Mitchell, without seeking Washington's sanction, agreed to enter into negotiations. Admiral Warren selected Attorney General Richard John Uniacke to represent the British interest. Uniacke was also Advocate General in the Court of Vice Admiralty, and besides making a fortune in fees from acting for the Crown in the numerous prize cases coming before the court, he was thoroughly familiar with Admiralty law. Although Mitchell understood Uniacke to be "a character of high standing," he was also reputed to be "violent in his enmity" to the United States.[50] As it turned out, Mitchell would later report that Uniacke had "been perfectly polite in his Manners with Me, nothing on the subject of Politicks has passed except what related to the immediate Business we were upon."[51] Representing Great Britain with Uniacke was Lieutenant William Miller. They began work in the third week of November, and within a week Mitchell could write to James Monroe that arrangements were in a form that would be ready for his examination.

There seems to have been little disagreement. On 28 November the parties signed an agreement, or "cartel" as it was officially called, with 13 articles.[52] Article 1 described the tariff of values attached to various ranks, from an admiral or general, who could be exchanged for an officer of equal rank or for 60 other prisoners, down to a common seaman or soldier, who could be exchanged one for one. Article 2 defined surgeons, pursers, chaplains, schoolmasters and civilians as non-combatants, who were to be released without exchange and were not to be imprisoned. Article 3 dealt with the ports in the respective countries where prisoners were to be brought for exchange.

Articles 4, 5 and 6 laid out conditions of parole. Normally all commissioned army and naval officers were placed on parole and provided with a daily living allowance paid by the government granting the parole. At British insistence, as a means of discouraging privateering, the Halifax agreement allowed parole only for captains and first and second lieutenants of privateers with 14 or more carriage guns that mounted four-pound shot. Mitchell, who had argued for a ten-gun limit — which would have encompassed the vast majority of American privateers — had to give way when Admiral Warren stated that he had no authority to go below British European practice. Those on parole signed a form detailing the conditions of their parole. If violated, the offender was "liable to be dealt with according to the usages and customs observed in such cases, by the most civilized Nations, when at war."

As the Halifax Agreement was provisional, Article 13 provided for its submission to the respective governments for ratification. In forwarding the document to Washington, Mitchell

Portrait of Richard John Uniacke by Robert Field. As he was senior law officer of the Crown in Nova Scotia, Admiral Sir John Warren gave Uniacke the task of negotiating with John Mitchell, American agent, an agreement for the exchange of prisoners.

told Secretary of the Navy, Paul Hamilton, that he felt "gratified" in making it and he believed it was "the first on general principles that the United States ever made."[53]

Within days of his arrival in Washington, Colonel Thomas Barclay (a loyalist officer who had settled in Nova Scotia and afterwards been appointed British Consul General at New York), who had been named as British agent for prisoners of war in the United States, reported to the Transport Board that President James Madison had not ratified the Halifax agreement and had

During the early morning hours of 13 October 1812, American troops crossed the Niagara River with the aim of capturing the strategic Queenston Heights. Although the Americans initially seized the heights, a valiant charge of redcoats drove them off. Hundreds of Americans were captured, some of whom were sent to Melville Island.

proposed some alterations.[54] A major issue for the Americans related to Article 7, which stated that prisoners were to be allowed "a sufficient subsistence." Barclay argued that though the clause was vague, it should stand as written. The Americans, however, insisted in describing what rations would be provided prisoners in great detail and drafted a second version, dated 13 May 1813, which Barclay sent to the Transport Board.

The board drafted another version and sent it to Barclay with instructions to propose it for acceptance in lieu of the previous draft, especially noting that "no Alteration can be made in the Rations at present allowed to American Prisoners of War either in this country [Britain] or on Foreign Stations [such as Halifax and Bermuda]...."[55] The Transport Board's version was never printed. Neither the Halifax nor the Washington Agreement was ever ratified by both governments, but they remained informally in force.

Exchanges Under the Halifax and Washington Agreements

The Halifax and Washington agreements focused generally on arrangements for exchanging prisoners. Both laid out a system of equivalency based on rank and service, with a table of values. Officers and other ranks could be exchanged one for one, or for a number of seamen or private soldiers, as determined by the table of values. If either nation at any time had delivered more prisoners than it had received, it could stop sending further prisoners until the imbalance was rectified. This provision was to prove particularly difficult for the Americans because the balance of captured prisoners was usually in favour of the British.

At Halifax, it was comparatively easy to know at all times the number and rank of prisoners, so that lists for exchange could be prepared from the General Entry Book kept by Lieutenant William Miller. Such was not the case in the United States, where British prisoners were held in custody in scattered ports along the eastern seaboard and at inland locations. After the American government appointed John Mason as commissary general of prisoners and Thomas Barclay's arrival as British Agent in May 1813, they became the final authority for prisoner exchanges. It could take months before there would be agreement on the lists of prisoners to be exchanged.

In practice, at Halifax the admiral on the North American Station made the final decision on prisoner exchanges and the transfer of prisoners to Dartmoor in England to deal with overcrowding. John Mitchell took the position that he had the right to select which American prisoners held on Melville Island or on parole were to be exchanged, but actually William Miller determined the selection with the final authority being the admiral on station in his capacity as commander-in-chief. Although the Admiralty had instructed Admiral Sawyer that American privateer prisoners were to be considered on an equal footing with naval and army prisoners, they were the last to be selected for exchange and the first to be sent to Dartmoor as a means of keeping them from returning to privateering.

Shortly after John Mitchell arrived at Halifax, Admiral Warren wrote him that he had given Miller authority to select 300 prisoners to be sent by a cartel, without mentioning any conditions for an exchange.[56] Generally, in this early period of the war, the American government left Mitchell to arrange what exchanges he could, but he was hindered by the failure of district marshals in ports along the eastern American seaboard to forward British prisoners to be exchanged at Halifax. In February 1813, he sent a circular to the marshals of various districts calling on them to forward their prisoners because of the great number of Americans imprisoned at Halifax.[57] Even after the appointment of John Mason as commissary of prisoners, Mitchell reported that the prisoners complained bitterly, for they were told they would be sent home as soon as a cartel vessel arrived, but Mason had not sent him any information about the arrival of cartels.[58]

In May 1813, the number of American prisoners began increasing rapidly. A committee of prisoners reported regularly to Mitchell on the numbers victualled with small stores (soap and such like). On 4 May it reported a figure of 505.[59] By the summer of 1813, William Miller informed Mitchell that the balance stood against the Americans upwards of 1,100 prisoners and he had in custody another 600.[60]

United States Army Prisoners to Melville Island

At the beginning of the war British strategy for the defence of Canada against an expected American invasion was to concentrate the bulk of regular troops available at Quebec and Montreal and to await reinforcements from Britain. Major General Isaac Brock had only 1,600 regulars with which to defend Upper Canada along its 600-mile border with the United States. General William Hull, an elderly veteran of the American War of Independence whose orders were to conquer Canada, assembled his forces, which consisted of more than

2,500 men and 33 cannon, at Fort Detroit. Nevertheless, Brock decided to capture the fort with 300 regulars, 400 militia and 600 Native warriors. By convincing the Americans that his force was much larger and playing on fears of an Indian massacre, Brock persuaded Hull to surrender on 16 August. He lacked the troops to guard all the captured men, so he paroled 1,600 Ohio militiamen on the provision that they not fight again until they could be exchanged with an equal number of British soldiers who had been captured. General Hull, his officers and the regulars were sent by ship to Quebec. To accommodate them, Sir George Prevost, commander-in-chief and Governor General, had a vessel purchased to be used as a prison ship. The American government appointed Colonel Gardner as its agent at Quebec.

The next American invasion attempt took place in October 1812, when 6,000 troops, half of whom were regulars, were assembled on the Unites States side of the Niagara River. Opposing them were Brock's force of 600 regulars, an equal number of militia and 250 Six Nations warriors under war chiefs John Norton and Joseph Brant. The American commander, Major General Stephen Van Rensselaer's plan was to seize the strategic Queenston Heights. The crossing took place on the night of 12 – 13 October. In the battle that followed, Brock was killed, but the result was a decisive British victory, with the Americans driven back across the river. A total of 500 Americans were killed or wounded. Another 456 regulars and 489 militiamen surrendered. As at Fort Detroit, the lack of transport and rations caused the British to parole at least the militiamen. Those not paroled were sent to Quebec.

In the spring of 1813, more Americans were captured as the result of the battles of Stoney Creek, Beaver Dam, Chateauguay and Crysler's Farm. Generally, their condition was deplorable. Many of them had received little training, especially the conscripted militiamen, before being committed to battle, and they had been led by incompetent officers. They had suffered greatly from being issued summer clothing when they needed winter outfits. Poor hygiene had resulted in much illness, and the attempted invasions during 1812 and 1813 had been defeated, which did nothing to improve morale.

Conditions aboard the prison ships were unhealthy, and there were complaints over rations. These caused Sir George Prevost to send to Melville Island as many prisoners as shipping allowed. Crews from British merchant vessels, however, had been pressed to serve with the British fleet on the Great Lakes. To provide for their replacement to man the vessels carrying the prisoners to Halifax, Prevost ordered that American prisoners, if they could not be induced to serve aboard the vessels, be forced to serve. Although the prisoners refused, considering it unjust, they were forced on board by British press gangs. By the end of 1813 nearly 1,000 American soldiers had been sent to Melville Island.

An alarmed Lieutenant-Governor Sherbrooke reported that there were 1,654 prisoners at Melville Island. To ensure their safe custody he was obliged to keep a very strong detachment of troops constantly on duty. He requested more troops, but because prisoners would be sent to England as early as possible in the spring, Lord Bathurst, the Secretary of State for War and the Colonies, refused the request for immediate reinforcements.[61]

Such was the concern caused by the rising number of prisoners and a small garrison, that Miller began assuring prisoners that they would soon be free from their confinement and sent home, though the British planned to ship as many as possible to England if vessels could be found for the task. The authorities did everything they could to keep the prisoners quiet, while increasing the presence of troops on Melville Island to deal with any uprising. When shipping was available, Miller would select the number to be sent to England and let those selected believe that they were going home. Such was the security that the prisoners did not find out about the deception until they were taken by boat to a British warship and placed in the lower deck. Benjamin Waterhouse well remembered how he and others were completely misled by the turnkey John Grant and Miller into believing they were being sent home when their destination was, in fact, the dreaded Dartmoor.[62]

When, in October 1813, Admiral Warren proposed an exchange as a means of reducing the number of prisoners, Mitchell replied that he could not proceed until he had heard from Washington, to avoid "a double exchange," and that a plan should be adopted to release a majority of the American prisoners detained at the Halifax Station.[63] From Washington, John Mason blamed Mitchell for the problems arising over arranging exchanges. He had found Mitchell's lists of prisoners incomplete and had to apply to Thomas Barclay, who received monthly reports from British agents. Mason ordered Mitchell to provide monthly reports. Nonetheless, Mason told Mitchell that he had been right to refuse exchanges that were not authorized by himself and Barclay.[64]

Rising Apprehensions

More prisoners arrived from Quebec in October and November. By late autumn Warren, faced with rising fears in Halifax and with no exchanges arranged, began putting prisoners on merchant vessels sailing to England. Sherbrooke again had written Bathurst in December on the "impolicy and inconvenience" of continuing to use Halifax as a depot for American prisoners of war, recommending either Pictou or Louisbourg as less objectionable places. If the prisoners remained at Halifax, the Melville Prison would have to be enlarged. The decision reached, however, was to send prisoners to England at every opportunity.[65]

Exchanges were renewed, but the imbalance in numbers remained. In June 1814, for example, the British cartel *Matilda* arrived in Salem, Massachusetts with 350 Americans for exchange, but returned with only 140 British prisoners. At the same time, the British continued to send hundreds of prisoners from Halifax to England on, in Mitchell's words, "the plea of thinning the Prison." The crews of privateers were chiefly selected because, in Mitchell's opinion, "the object [was] for to harass and distress that description of prisoners."

After Captain John Cochet succeeded William Miller as British Agent at Halifax in May 1814, he continued the policy of selecting the American prisoners for cartels. He informed Mitchell that he could not permit him "to interfere in selecting prisoners of war in his [Cochet's] custody."[66] Finally, in mid-1814, Mason made representations on the issue to Thomas Barclay. Barclay apparently wrote to the admiral on the Halifax Station. However, there is no evidence that authorities at Halifax changed the policy.[67] When a further 600 prisoners were sent to Britain, Mitchell concluded that they intended to keep few prisoners at Melville Island, and their policy would be to ship more prisoners to England by every available convoy.[68] He found it very disturbing that he was unable to stop the practice, which he considered to be in direct violation of both the Halifax and Washington provisional agreements.

Hundreds more American prisoners began arriving at Halifax as the result of British operations along the eastern American seaboard and in Canada. In August 1814 a British force under the command of Vice Admiral Sir Alexander Cochrane landed near Washington and defeated

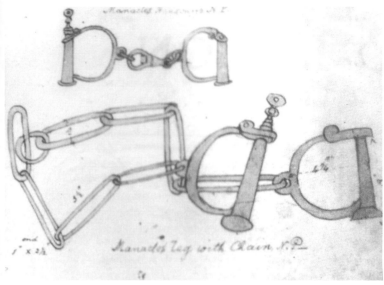

The USS Chesapeake *carried such manacles as pictured here to use in the expectation of defeating the* Shannon, *only to have them used on themselves by the* Shannon's *crew.*

an American army at the Battle of Bladensburg. The American government fled the capital and the British burnt a number of buildings. However, the Americans put up much stronger resistance when the British attempted unsuccessfully to capture Baltimore. General Robert Ross, the commander of the British land forces, was killed. His body was brought back to Halifax for burial in St. Paul's Cemetery. Only 25 of the American prisoners taken in these operations were sent to Halifax, with the others probably sent to Bermuda.

In September, a British combined force assembled off Shelburne on Nova Scotia's south shore to launch a surprise attack on Moose Island in Passamaquoddy Bay. When the force arrived at the island, Captain Sir Thomas Hardy summoned Major Putnam, commander of the garrison, to surrender in five minutes. Putman refused, but after consulting with his officers, the flag was struck. Putnam and his officers were paroled, but the garrison of 80 men was sent to Halifax. In the Melville Island Entry Book, they are described as United States Sea Fencibles — companies formed for the defence of harbours. Operations continued with the capture of Machias and Castine further down the Maine coast. The invading force encountered so little resistance that only six prisoners were sent to Melville Island.

The major influx of prisoners came from Canada. Nearly 400 arrived, mostly in September. By the end of that month Captain Cochet told Mitchell that the British held 3,000 more prisoners than the number of British prisoners held by the United States.[69] He would allow non-combatants and some of those on parole, but no prisoners of war, to return on a cartel that had not brought British prisoners. The Americans, desperate to rectify the imbalance, offered a bounty of $100 a prisoner to privateers to hand over captured prisoners for exchange instead of releasing them on a neutral shore. All Mitchell could report was that there was no further hope of Americans being returned until the imbalance had been rectified. This would not happen before peace came in 1815.[70]

USS Chesapeake Prisoners

The famous battle between HMS *Shannon*, under the command of Captain Philip Broke, and the USS *Chesapeake*, commanded by Captain James Lawrence, that took place outside Boston Harbour on 1 June 1813 was one of the quickest and bloodiest ship-to-ship actions on record — eleven minutes elapsed between the firing of the first gun and the boarding of the *Chesapeake*, and in four more minutes she surrendered.[71] Lawrence was mortally wounded. His last order was "Tell the men to fire faster! Don't give up the ship!" Three hundred and seventeen prisoners were taken and manacled with the handcuffs the *Chesapeake* had brought with her in anticipation of British prisoners. The *Shannon* returned to Halifax with the *Chesapeake* on 6 June, and the wounded were taken to the Naval Hospital. William Swift, a surgeon's mate aboard *Chesapeake*, wrote a friend in Boston on 8 June of the wounded all being in the hospital, which was "superior to any I have ever seen."[72] Lieutenant George Budd, the senior surviving officer of *Chesapeake*, and a number of midshipmen were sent to Dartmouth on parole, while the remainder of the prisoners were taken to Melville Island.

The case of the *Chesapeake* prisoners is a good example of the complexity of prisoner exchanges, compounded by communication delays among the parties involved — John Mason and Thomas Barclay; Mason and Mitchell; Mason and various marshals in American ports responsible for British prisoners; and Miller and Mitchell in Halifax. At the time of battle the British cartel *Agnes* was already at sea on her way to Boston with 125 prisoners she had taken aboard in Halifax. On arrival at Boston *Agnes* handed over her prisoners and took aboard 133 British prisoners for a return voyage to Halifax. Meanwhile, an American merchantman, *Frederick Augustus*, had been captured as a prize and taken to Halifax. The Court of Vice Admiralty, however, declared that the vessel was not a legal prize and she was restored to her owners.

After *Shannon* arrived with *Chesapeake*, the *Frederick Augustus*'s owners were required to provide passage to Boston for 64 officers, seamen and marines, of whom 61 were from the *Chesapeake*.[73] She left on 25 June. Next, *Agnes* returned to Halifax, where she took aboard about 35 American prisoners, of whom 13 were from *Chesapeake*, and then sailed for Boston, where she arrived in August.

Meanwhile, Captain James Lawrence of the *Chesapeake* was buried on 8 June, with every honour due his rank and bravery. His coffin was covered with the American colours and escorted by captains of the Royal Navy. The procession, led by a band, marched through the streets to St. Paul's Cemetery. Several wounded American officers attended. Five days later Lieutenant Augustus Ludlow died and was buried near his captain. However, some Republican papers stated that Lawrence's burial was performed in Halifax "as a cruel mockery and insult."[74] Captain George Crowninshield Jr. decided to try and bring Lawrence's body back to the United States. He requested President Madison's authority to travel at his own expense to Halifax in the brig *Henry*, "to procure and bring to his native land, the remains of the fallen hero, Captain JAMES LAWRENCE, that he may be interred with those funeral honors to which his character is so eminently entitled."[75] He received permission to sail under a flag of truce with the necessary documents to procure the body.

Henry sailed from Salem on 7 August with a crew of 12 privateer captains and passed Sambro Lighthouse on 10 August. At 11 o'clock she came to anchor under York Redoubt. William Miller had heard of *Henry*'s mission and he came on board, took the vessel's passport and returned to Halifax. During *Henry*'s stay in Halifax, an officer and a file of marines were posted aboard, and no one except Captain Crowninshield was allowed ashore. However, the crew was treated with much politeness and attention by the officers at the fort, and by the officers who visited the ship.[76] At midnight on 12 August, Miller came alongside with the remains of Captain Lawrence and Lieutenant Ludlow, with express orders for the *Henry* to get underway immediately. Such had been the secrecy that *Henry* had been unable to obtain any Halifax newspapers, but her crew did record vessels seen and their armament and noted that the privateer *Growler* had been captured off Cape Race.

After *Henry's* return to Salem the bodies were conveyed ashore with impressive ceremonies. The organizers had wanted to use the largest meetinghouse in town, but were refused, ostensibly because it could only be used for public worship, though the real reason was the divisions over the war.[77] The wishes of Lawrence's family to have him buried in New York were met, and his final resting place is Trinity Church burial ground, New York City.

Seven officers and seamen from the *Chesapeake* also returned aboard *Henry*. John Mitchell thought he had reached an understanding that all the remaining *Chesapeake* officers were to be sent home, as well as the sick and wounded, as soon as shipping could be found. He wrote Mason that he believed the British had not returned them because of the American detention of 12 men from the captured British frigate, *Guerriere*. At this point, General Mason intervened to stop the *Agnes* from taking on board more than 35 British prisoners who were also to be only sick and wounded as part of the exchange for those from *Chesapeake*. Mason ordered *Agnes* detained, but the order did not reach the marshals until the vessel had taken on British prisoners at Portsmouth and at Portland for exchange at Halifax. When her captain found his vessel detained, he slipped out of the harbour clandestinely. Although fired on by shore forts, *Agnes* returned undamaged to Halifax. Meanwhile, at Halifax, as part of the ongoing retaliation and counter retaliation involving the taking of hostages (see below) the British authorities had placed in the Halifax gaol six privateer officers and ten seamen from the *Chesapeake*. There seems to have been no further exchange involving *Chesapeake* officers and seamen until August 1814, when the cartel *Perseverance* arrived at Providence Rhode Island with 266 American prisoners, of whom 103 were from the *Chesapeake*.[78]

Portrait of Captain George Crowninshield Jr., the privateer captain who organized the return of the body of Captain James Lawrence to the United States.

CHAPTER 3

"THIS DAY WE EMBARK'D FOR HELL"

A prisoner poor and out of sight
Confined from all enjoyment
Doom'd through the day & endless nights
To live without employment
On Melville Island doom'd to be
By Centinels surrounded
My home, my bed, a prison deck
My heart with anguish wounded.
But soon I hope for sweet release
In realms of splendid glory
In scenes of love in bowers of peace
Where glows the blest Aurora.
Composed by a Soldier on Melville Island[1]

As with the French prisoners, the prison staff provided each American prisoner on arrival with a hammock and blankets and then the boatswain divided them into their messes with "The Whites ... separate from the blacks — And Yankee lads from Monsieur Jacks [French]—."[2] It is unknown how many prisoners were black because the Entry Book made no mention of race.

The prisoners' day began at sunrise when John Grant, the turnkey, opened the prison barracks door and called, "turn out, all out." Each man lashed up his hammock and carried it into the yard for roll call. The night tub was carried out and washed and windows were opened. Cooks from each of the messes then went to the cookhouse to prepare coffee. All meals were eaten in barracks. The prison was swept out twice a week with prisoners of each mess taking turns. When the prison was washed, prisoners were kept outside — in all weathers — until the floors had completely dried. According to Benjamin Waterhouse, Lieutenant Miller paid great attention to cleanliness and to the men's clothes. Those who did not conform, Miller sent to the black hole under the prison barracks, in solitary confinement, on bread and water for up to ten days. For this the prisoners applauded him. Waterhouse noted that those prisoners who had formerly been intemperate were the worst when it came to personal cleanliness.[3]

According to Transport Board regulations, prison officials provided daily rations of one pound of bread, one pound of beef and a gill (a quarter pint) of peas. With funds sent to him via a London bank, John Mitchell provided — through William Sutherland, the prison steward — a sufficiency of coffee, sugar, potatoes and tobacco and such items as soap.[4] He also sent money to a prisoners' committee to be given to prisoners so that they could purchase such items as candy, apples, lobsters, smoked herring and rich spruce beer. Some prisoners operated canteens. Apparently, one prisoner found a way to counterfeit Spanish dollars, which circulated widely within the prison and also found their way into Halifax, resulting in a government notice appearing in the *Weekly Chronicle* warning citizens to be on guard for the counterfeit

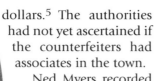

dollars.[5] The authorities had not yet ascertained if the counterfeiters had associates in the town.

Ned Myers recorded that he commenced gaming operations by purchasing shares in a dice-board, a *vingt-et-un* table and a quino table.[6] He and a fellow prisoner also set up a shop from which they sold smoked herrings, pipes, tobacco, cigars, spruce beer and — when it could be smuggled into the prison — rum. Their trade lasted throughout the winter of 1813–14 when the prison population numbered more than 1500.

Gambling was the chief occupation of most prisoners, with backgammon being the favourite game of chance. When the inevitable fights broke out, the "boxers" were thrown into the black hole. Dancing to the fiddle was also a popular pastime. Conversation among the prisoners centred around news of exchanges and the sailing of cartels — their greatest fear was that they would not be exchanged, but sent instead to the dreaded Dartmoor. Until the evening, prisoners were left to their own devices. Before locking them in the barracks the turnkeys held a roll call, then they barred the door. Once in their hammocks the prisoners spent the time telling stories and singing songs until the 9 o'clock gun signal.[7] On the first night he was shut up, Benjamin Waterhouse, however, could not sleep because of noise from every hammock. He graphically described his distress:

> Some were lamenting their hard fate at being shut up…. Some were cursing and execrating their oppressors; others lamenting their aberrations from rectitude, and *disobedience to parents, and head strong wilfulness, that drove them to sea, contrary to their parents wish, while others of the younger class, were sobbing out their lamentations at the thoughts of what their mothers and sisters suffered, after knowing of their imprisonment. Not infrequently the whole night was spent in this way….*[8]

To celebrate the fourth of July, 1814, the prisoners strung a pendant from one barrack room to another. In the middle of the room they suspended a piece of cloth on which there was a painting of American naval victories in the war and an emblem of Liberty standing on a lion with a spear in her hand. They kept the day by dancing and drinking water, because they could not get any rum. But their situation did not permit them to rejoice as if they had their liberty.[9]

Halifax clergy also held divine services on Sundays. Many of the people from Halifax who came out to visit on Sundays apparently were Loyalists, whom Benjamin Waterhouse claimed came "to gratify their eyes, instead of going to a place of worship, with sight of what they called 'rebels.'"[10]

Prisoners' Justice

Once a week, after the prisoners were locked in their barracks, an individual named as "Moderator" called them to order. They would then elect a "President," a new "Moderator" and a "Tub Inspector" for the ensuing week.[11] At Dartmoor, a prisoners' committee drafted "Regulations established by the Committee appointed by the Magority [sic] of the Prisoners," which established rules for behaviour among the prisoners and the punishments for breaking them.[12] A similar set of rules seems to have been in place at Melville Island, because presidents did call into being courts with juries to try

Above: Melville Island from the North East *by J.E. Woolford in 1817. He exercised some artistic licence by giving the prison building an extra row of windows. Of the Melville Island views he painted this is considered his best.* Left: *Privateersman Benjamin Palmer of Stonington, Connecticut whose diary remains an importance source for prisoner life on Melville Island.*

prisoners accused of offences. In the Dartmoor regulations any person found guilty of "Treachery, Thief [sic], or uncleanlyness shall receive corperal punishment" as a jury should decide.[13] Flogging was also the punishment for theft at Melville Prison. The poem composed by a prisoner on Melville Island described one such trial, in which the accused was found guilty of theft — "A crime both mean and filthy"— and for which the punishment was two dozen lashes with a cat of nine tails:

The Cat is brought, he streight is bound
And A huge crowd is gather'd round
He's stript his back receives the lashes
He groans, he screams, he kicks &
  Thrashes
His mutilated body shews
The purple seams of cuting [sic] blows
Their sport being done they straight
  unbind him
He runs nor dares to look behind him
The wicked flee when none pursue
While upright men stand firm and
  true.[14]

Above: In war, Halifax's dockyard was critical for the Royal Navy's operations in the North Atlantic. It also played an essential role in outfitting Nova Scotian privateers. Right: A drawing of a cat of nine tails.

At Dartmoor one man was sentenced by his fellow prisoners to 500 lashes for stealing £10. Cooks could receive 18 lashes for skimming the fat off the soup for their own use. As at Melville Island, most of the American prisoners at Dartmoor were seamen and privateers; the punishments dealt out in prison courts were similar to those imposed by their own officers when at sea.

Escapes

Of the 63 American prisoners who ran away from the Naval Hospital in Halifax, from Melville Prison, from parole or from a citizen who was employing them, 20 were retaken.[15] A higher number of Americans were recaptured compared to the French prisoners who had escaped before them because of much tighter security at Melville Prison and a more aggressive pursuit of escapees after the War of 1812 began. Also, the punishment for recaptured prisoners could be severe. Mitchell reported to John Mason that two

American officers had been confined for at least 13 days "in dark cells, dressed by way of degradation in yellow cloaths [sic] and chained to a 9-lb shot, because they had attempted to escape."[16]

When Mitchell protested, correctly, that the 13 days exceeded the limit of 10 days in the Halifax Agreement, Miller told him the reason was that one of the prisoners had declared he would escape if ever the occasion offered. In fact, he did escape again, but was retaken and placed in irons. Mitchell reported to Mason that he would complain of such treatment, but he considered it useless because Miller was acting on instructions, and the admiral was at sea.[17] Thomas Swain underwent similar treatment for attempting to escape. He wrote Mitchell of how he was brought out of the dungeon clothed in a yellow suit with a shackle to his leg and exposed as a common spectacle to the whole guard of soldiers drawn up for that purpose.[18]

The first successful American escape on record

was made by Moses Burbank, a privateer commander on parole, and two others on 10 November 1813.[19] They were suspected of having secreted themselves on board neutral vessels bound for the United States. In August 1814, 11 privateers escaped from Melville Island and reached Halifax, where they attempted to carry off a boat, but were discovered. Five were recaptured, one apparently drowned, and the remainder got away. As punishment for not informing on the escapees, their messmates' beef ration was stopped. John Mitchell believed that the escapees made the attempt because they feared being sent to England and Dartmoor.[20]

After his successful escape and return to Salem in September, Edmund Upton claimed that this was his third successful escape from Melville Island prison accomplished by seizing a boat and sailing it to Machias.[21] The facts were somewhat different. Upton was first captured as a steward on the privateer *Revenge* on 4 December 1812. He escaped from the Naval Hospital on 27 July 1813 and was not retaken. He then joined the privateer *Lizard*, which was captured on 5 March 1814 and the crew sent to Melville Island. He escaped on 8 May 1814 but was retaken eight days later. Presumably he was duly punished, but this did not deter him as he escaped again on 10 August and arrived back in Salem in September.[22] Later, in October, four seamen escaped by cutting through the prison barracks' floor, but local militia recaptured all of them. It was worth their while because each soldier received a guinea for each prisoner captured.

In late 1814, the prisoners hatched a grand conspiracy. The conspirators planned to subdue their guards and seize Fort George on Citadel Hill, which commanded Halifax town and harbour. Then — in Ned Myers' words — the 1,800 prisoners (his number) would "go off in triumph." As Myers described it, initially 50 prisoners entered into the plan, which included the digging of a tunnel.

They first broke through the floor into one of the black-hole cells and used a large mess chest to conceal the operation. Working in gangs of six, they passed up the dirt they had dug out and put it in night tubs, which were emptied every morning in the Northwest Arm. After two months they had dug a passage wide enough for two abreast, some 20 or 30 yards long, and were nearly ready to come to the surface. They then began recruiting and enlisted about 400 men in the scheme, each of whom was sworn to secrecy. However, they were betrayed, it was believed, by one of their own number.[23]

Privateer officers who were housed in the upper deck of the barracks had entered into the scheme. They had communicated by lifting up the floor between the decks after the prisoners had been locked in for the night. When the British learned of the privateer officers' involvement, they sent nearly all of them to Dartmoor in a draft of 600. Those left at Melville Island found themselves too well watched to plan any more escapes. Even conversation at night was prohibited.

Prisoners and Agents

The overwhelming desire of Melville Island prisoners was to be listed for exchange and not sent to Dartmoor. Their anguished pleas to John Mitchell to act on their behalf have survived in numerous letters found in his papers. Cartels brought letters from their families, many of whom were destitute and in great distress. William Miller examined prisoners' letters, which Mitchell believed was not permitted by the Halifax Agreement and was done

There were two brigs named Diomede *of Salem, one a merchant vessel and the other a privateer of the Crowninshield family. In May 1813, HMS* La Hogue *captured the merchant vessel sailing from Manila for Salem loaded with indigo, sugar, redwood, tea and Indian corn. The crew were sent to Melville Island. As a prize she earned £178 for her captors. On 28 May 1814 off Sydney, HMS* Rifleman *captured the privateer* Dolphin, *John Crowninshield, captain, with a crew of 32. As a prize she earned £82. Until her capture, the* Dolphin *had sent many prizes into Salem. A month earlier John Crowninshield had been publicly thanked in a New York newspaper by officers of His Majesty's 65th Regiment for forwarding to them, unopened, several letters from Surinam, which the fortune of war had placed in his hands.*

by Miller "to mark his power."[24] American instructions for keeping prisoners, however, required that all letters of British prisoners be examined and that breaches of the rule be punished by stern measures.[25]

Miller also insisted that he or another official be present when Mitchell visited Melville Prison. Mitchell protested that the Halifax Agreement allowed him to visit the prisoners and "hear in private their complaints," because a "prisoner will readily tell his grievance if he has any to the person his government confides in if alone with him, but will be silent in the presence of Gaoler."[26] He asked James Monroe that he not be required to submit to Miller's interference in his duty to hear prisoners' complaints or to have every note from prisoners "opened, scribbled on and marked Examined." Miller, however, continued to examine all letters and informed Mitchell that prisoners were not to receive or send any letters whatever, except through his, Miller's hands, that they may be read and approved by him.[27]

Aside from pleas to Mitchell to have them exchanged, the prisoners' chief complaint was lack of clothing, which it was Mitchell's responsibility to supply. Numerous individuals wrote of their need for clothing. Joseph Livery, for example, wrote of how he and others of a privateer crew had been absent from their homes for nine months and in desperate need of clothes as they were "almost naked."[28] Hundreds of others required clothing, especially after the British begun sending soldiers captured in battles on the Canadian frontier to Melville Prison. In August 1813, Miller wrote to Mitchell that 400–500 were in desperate need. As winter approached that year, Miller wrote again of the necessity of supplying 1,500 prisoners with "the necessaries of life, namely jackets and trousers, shoes and stockings" and accused Mitchell of "a cruel neglect" of near 1,000 of them "having suffered to go barefooted, and otherwise miserably clad."[29] The author of a poem composed on Melville Island included nearly a whole page of verse on the subject of clothing, a few lines of which went:

> Because the weather calls for cloths
> To keep their hides from being froze —
> Lately a freight of cloaths arrive.
> The men flock, round like bees unhived —
> The Steward serves the Naked greedy —
> Objects of pity hear their wants ...[30]

When an Englishman on his way home from the United States stopped at Halifax in early November 1813, he was pressed by American masters of merchant vessels to visit Melville Island prison. He was told that very many prisoners had died and the hospital was now filled "with poor creatures whose complaints are generally brought on by want of clothing."[31] He found that the hospital was "absolutely filled with mere skeletons of men in all stages of consumption."[32] He enquired of the surgeons and nurses how they accounted for this dreadful situation. They all replied that it originated from want of comfortable clothing and that 50 had already died of consumption. When he walked through the prison with William Miller, the prisoners' requests for shoes, stockings and other forms of clothing were innumerable, though the most pressing demands had been met. The Englishman, who did not wish his name to appear in public, wrote a letter to the New York *Mercantile Advertiser*, saying that there was "very bad management everywhere" and he hoped that the publication of his letter might induce the proper department of American government "to relieve the distresses of these most unfortunate men, whose miseries must increase as the cold weather comes on."[33]

Mitchell had been dealing with individual

requests for clothing by arranging for the prison steward, William Sutherland, to either purchase the required clothing or advance cash to the prisoners for the prison tailors to produce the items. But Mitchell was unable to make large purchases because of the difficulties he had in obtaining the necessary funds. Apparently his bills on the United States government were not being accepted in Halifax, though Miller disputed that this was a problem. Mitchell had turned to a Halifax merchant, John Osborn, who agreed to give credit for $5,000 on Mitchell's note being accepted in Washington.[34] The anonymous letter writer to the *Mercantile Advertiser* said that Miller had advanced Mitchell $12,000 for the purchase of clothing. Almost certainly his letter caused the American government to ship by cartel 24 boxes of specie to the value of $12,000 to Halifax in December 1813 to meet Mitchell's demands for funds.[35] Miller had already supplied hundreds of items of clothing and billed Mitchell.[36]

When visiting the prison Mitchell arrived in a carriage. According to Benjamin Palmer, as soon as he arrived at the barracks' door "everyone pays him proper respect by pulling off their hats, he walks along to hear the news[,] everyone has some grievance to relate and the old gentleman answers each one in turn."[37] Palmer himself asked for clothes. Mitchell delivered letters and newspapers to prisoners frantic for news of their families. William Miller, however, was not impressed with Mitchell's conduct, at least on one visit in the autumn of 1813. As usual Miller attended him with the purpose of replying to any complaints made by the prisoners. He asked Mitchell to visit the prison hospital and the prison ship. He also offered to muster the prisoners so that Mitchell might ascertain their condition.[38] However, Mitchell declined, saying that he could not stay long, but then spent a considerable time with the officers living in the upper deck of the prison building, who Miller said were not in immediate need of anything.

Miller seems to have been correct about the officers. An officer using only the initials J.T. wrote his parents that he was in a perfect state of health and enjoying himself, considering his confinement. The officers had a separate place from the rest of the prisoners, where they had a stove, which made them "quite comfortable." There were about 1,000 Americans, including those in hospital on the island. "Our living is very good," he said. "With what our government allows us, we have one pound of bread, one of beef, and plenty of potatoes; coffee, sugar, tobacco, soap and every thing that can be desired but our liberty."[39]

Mitchell's preference for the company of the officers did on one occasion result in insults from some boys during a visit. When this was discovered by the officers, they informed Mitchell that they had punished the boys and hoped that he would not discontinue his agreeable visits in future.[40] In July 1814, the officers of the upper deck wrote to Mitchell thanking him for the interest always manifested by him. They also particularly thanked him for his exertions, though futile, to prevent a number of prisoners being sent to England.[41]

Although the number of black seamen imprisoned at Melville Island is unknown, at Dartmoor hundreds of blacks were segregated in the upper storey of one of the barracks.[42] Some of them had probably initially been confined at Halifax. In his correspondence John Mitchell first mentions black prisoners in November 1812. He wrote the marshal in Boston that among 12 American prisoners he was sending two blacks — John and John L. Bullock, the property of the Navy Agent in Savannah, Georgia — asking him to forward them to the Navy Department in Washington, which would return them to their owner.[43] In March 1813, Mitchell reported to Washington that he had clothed and "claimed" four black men who had been part of the crew of the revenue cutter *James Madison*. He suspected that they were slaves from Georgia and wished for instructions from James Monroe on how to proceed if Admiral Warren refused to deliver them up to him.[44]

Within a few days of Mitchell making his request, William Miller informed him that the four had been liberated according to an act of parliament, presumably the 1807 Abolition Act that had abolished the slave trade.[45] Miller followed existing policy, which was to separate blacks from other prisoners and to refuse to give up either free blacks or slaves for exchange. Vice Admiral Sir John Warren ordered them sent to Bermuda. Mitchell asked James Monroe if the former slaves were now British subjects. He found the subject "a new and extraordinary one," and was afraid to interfere further without Monroe's instructions. Mitchell would have been aware of the orders given to British vessels then blockading Chesapeake Bay to receive any escaped slaves as free men. This was probably why he never again raised the issue of claiming blacks who he suspected of being slaves.

John Mitchell and American Smugglers

At the beginning of the war, Lieutenant-Governor Sherbrooke suspended certain laws governing British trade and introduced a licensing system to encourage the importation of American cargoes of provisions and naval stores. A British Order in

Above: Admiral Sir John Borlase Warren who served in various appointments at Halifax from 1807 to 1814.

Council followed in October 1812, which threw open the ports of Halifax, and Saint John and St. Andrews in New Brunswick to licensed trade from American ports. Provisions of all kinds, as well as such naval stores as turpentine and pitch, could be imported aboard American vessels into these three ports. American vessels could load cargoes of British and European goods and West Indian products, which they would then smuggle into the United States.

By this means, much-needed American provisions were shipped from Halifax to the British forces fighting Napoleon's army in Spain and to the Canadas. They were also used to victual the North Atlantic squadron blockading American ports. It is probable that much of the flour and beef provided to prisoners on Melville Island was American in origin. The British war effort in the Canadas could not have been maintained without provisions shipped from Halifax and, in winter, carried by sleigh from upper New York. As prize goods — many of which originally came from captured American vessels — accumulated in Halifax, another Order in Council in July 1813 allowed their export to the United States.

A favourite means of carrying out this massive illicit trade was for American vessels to sail under Danish or Swedish neutral flags. Shortly after his arrival at Halifax, Mitchell wrote the Boston port officials that "Your Boston Swedes continue to arrive weekly," and that "they change names."[46] He suggested that as they were coming two or three times a week — "the Yankee Gentry will trade no matter with who" — they could bring sealed correspondence.[47] Boston customhouse

A view of the establishments of Boston merchants, reputedly the financiers of the massive smuggling operations before and during the War of 1812.

officials requested Mitchell to provide information on which vessels arrived in Halifax, from what port and what methods the violators used to evade American laws. Mitchell replied that those concerned with the illegal traffic were careful that he saw none of them, and their Halifax friends were "jealous to the highest degree" of all who visited him lest these persons should communicate who was involved in the smuggling.[48]

Some officers of *Chesapeake* were initially allowed to live in Halifax, in one case with family friends. However, in August 1813 the officers were summarily sent to Dartmouth and Preston. No reason was given to Mitchell for this "rigor" towards the crew of the *Chesapeake*, but he was persuaded it was related to the fear of the smugglers from the Unites States being seen and known.[49] There was little Halifax authorities could do about returning prisoners reporting on the extent of smuggling, whose stories were carried in numerous newspapers. An unnamed exchanged prisoner reported that at Halifax on one day 1300 barrels of flour had arrived and

large quantities had been coming in daily. He claimed that during the fall and spring of 1813 upwards of 20,000 barrels had been sent from Halifax to Quebec. Moreover, the authorities were sending beef, peas and every kind of produce raised in the United States to Quebec and other places in Canada.[50] He also stated he had heard British officers say that if the American government had prevented supplies *"from their friends in Boston"* and other places, the British provinces would have been in a state of starvation. Such a statement was not far from the truth. During September 1813, reputedly, in the course of a single day 17,000 barrels of flour and provisions arrived in Halifax.

A letter from an officer, again unnamed, headlined "TRADE WITH THE ENEMY" first appeared in the *Eastern Argus* in November 1813 and was then carried in other newspapers. The writer asked readers to join with him in exposing the nefarious traffic at present carried on under the Swedish flag.[51] They were:

> *… base and profligate enough to sell their country for filthy mammon — who, lost to all national feelings, can descend to the most humiliating conduct — to the most cringing servility of manners, and the most abject meanness, added to their avowed opposition of government, and open treasonable practices to obtain the slightest notice of the British government, in the person of their officers and agents … that there are at this moment, upwards of TWO HUNDRED men, who style themselves American Federalists, in the city of Halifax, in open and direct communication with G. Britain.*[52]

As well as smuggling provisions into Halifax in vessels navigated by Americans under the Swedish flag, the unnamed officer added that these scoundrels were smuggling silks into the United States in the form of bedding made up in mattresses. The figure of 200 Americans involved in smuggling in Halifax now became an official figure.[53]

In a similar case at New Haven, notices of libel were handed out on information coming directly from Halifax for five vessels and seven cargoes charged with smuggling. The *American Advocate* commented that Halifax "would appear by the course of trade, is becoming famous for the manufacture not only of dry goods and hard ware, but of rum, sugar and molasses in great abundance...."[54] So concerned were the Halifax authorities that some American prisoners, presumably waiting to be shipped out in a cartel, were confined by the Halifax authorities on transports in the harbour to prevent them from observing and recognizing the Americans involved in the vast smuggling trade between Halifax and New England.[55]

Mitchell also reported that the authorities had even suppressed the issue of a newspaper that had exposed the names of parties engaged in this licensed smuggling. As the months passed, Mitchell became more and more incensed over the smugglers and how smuggling had doubled the value of prizes and enriched the importers of British goods in Halifax. During 1813 more than 100 American vessels brought cargoes to Halifax and departed with British manufactures and such luxury goods as silks.

Toward the end of 1813, if not before, Mitchell began sending information on the identity of smugglers to American custom officials through exchanged prisoners. Knowledge of his conduct soon came to the notice of Thomas Jeffery, collector of customs at Halifax, who learned from a neutral brig that no less than ten licensed vessels carrying British and colonial manufactures and produce from Halifax, which had arrived in American ports, had been seized for trading with the enemy. The brig's master asserted that vessels were seized as a result of information that was sent from Halifax by Mitchell.[56]

William Miller and the American Prisoners

William Miller ran a tight ship. Benjamin Palmer described him as "old Jimy square foot ... stiff as a crow bar."[57] Benjamin Waterhouse claimed that Miller could have alleviated the suffering of the prisoners, especially by not making them stand out in all weathers while waiting for the washed floors of the barracks to dry.[58] Miller well knew the prisoners' dread of being sent to Dartmoor, and he did not hesitate to use it to gain their compliance. When, for example, some prisoners broke down the cookhouse door in a dispute over breakfast, he threatened to send them to England unless they behaved themselves.[59] Miller became noted among the prisoners for his rudeness and coarse language.[60] Miller's conduct and the conditions on Melville Island became part of a vitriolic debate, especially between Federalist newspapers that opposed the war and Republican papers that avidly supported it and President Madison. In late 1813, Miller wrote Mitchell that Thomas Barclay had been sending him paragraphs that were appearing in United States newspapers charging him with cruelty and ill-treatment toward the American Prisoners of War at Melville Island.[61] Although he considered them "as false as they are villainous," he feared that indifference to them would be eagerly grasped at and circulated as proof of his guilt. He called on Mitchell, as a man of honour, to enumerate specifically, every instance of cruelty and ill-treatment that the American agent had observed. Miller noted, in various printed extracts of Thomas Barclay's and Admiral Warren's correspondence with John Mason, passages of Mitchell's letters to the

American government that were critical of him.

Mitchell, for instance, had stated that no bedding had been supplied to the prisoners, which he must have known was false. Miller could only conclude that this and other incorrect statements were deliberate. In another example, Miller virtually accused Mitchell of lying. The American government had complained that two gentlemen by the names of Kirk and Hall had been confined in a Halifax gaol. The complaint was based on information provided by Mitchell, who claimed he had seen them there. However, Miller affirmed that they were never in gaol in Halifax, but were at Melville Island, where they lived with the officers, separate from the seamen, and were shown every indulgence in the few days they were imprisoned.

What Miller especially resented was an extract from a Portland paper that claimed Mitchell was not allowed to visit the American prisoners on Melville Island. Moreover, the paper stated that Miller "exercises every cruelty in his power."[62] In one reputed instance, when a man was absent during roll call, Miller immediately ordered the man next in line to be placed in the dungeon. Afterwards it was determined that the missing man had been dead for four days. As the prisoners underwent roll calls every morning and evening this tale was improbable. Another man was supposedly confined for 14 days on half-food allowance because he had advised one of the prisoners not to work.

In particular, it was reported that Miller often sneered at the prisoners' complaints and threatened them all dead, with the repeated expression, "You may die and be damned, the King has one hundred and fifty Acres of Land appropriated to bury you on." Miller fiercely resented this last charge and gave as his explanation that he had used the expression on a Sunday visit to the prison when he had observed that the prisoners were extremely dirty and he had

become "rather warm." He had told them not to blame him if they became sickly and that, "I have got 180 acres of the King's Ground to bury you in." Whatever words Miller actually used, they would come back to haunt him.

Benjamin Waterhouse recorded Miller's use of the same expression, but said that he had used it when the prisoners had protested the quality of the beef ration.[63] According to Waterhouse, Miller collected the prisoners and mounted the staircase of the prison building, which he used as a rostrum. He began a most passionate harangue, declaring that the beef was good enough and, "a d — d deal better that they had in their own country, and if they did not eat it, they should have none." Miller then continued to harangue the prisoners in language that showed the strained relationship that had developed between the prisoners and himself.

He called them damned scoundrels who had been begging and pleading him that they might be the first to be exchanged, so that they could return to their families, who were starving in their absence. They had been impudent, telling him that the King's beef was not good enough for their dainty stomachs. They had complained of ill-treatment, but he told them that they had never fared better in their lives. In His Majesty's royal prison, he told them sarcastically, they had everything "right and proper for persons taken fighting against his crown and dignity." There was a surgeon if they were sick and a hospital too. And if they should die, "there are boards enough (pointing to a pile of lumber in the yard) for to make you coffins, and an hundred and fifty acres of land to bury you in; and if you are not satisfied with all this, you may die and be d — d."[64] When he had finished this harangue Miller descended from his rostrum and strutted out of the prison yard, accompanied by hisses from some of the prisoners. However, the quality of beef improved — "full good enough for Mr.

Halifax was the main destination for American smugglers where American agricultural products and naval stores could be exchanged for British manufacturers to be in turn smuggled into the United States.

Miller himself to eat!"

Miller's words also appeared in the *Eastern Argus*, noted for its vilification of the British, as part of an article relating to the "disgusting particulars" of the place where 1,200 Americans (an accurate figure) were confined.[65] Melville Island, it said, was generally a very unhealthy situation and on this "nauseous spot" was a building of two storeys in which an upper room, 30 feet in length, was set apart for the sick. In the remainder of the upper part were 180 prisoners, while in the lower room there were, "770 more cooped up to breathe the same breath and generate disease by this narrow confine." On board a prison ship there were 350 more. A pestilence was carrying off three or four a day, said the article and then quoted part of Miller's "to die and be damned" speech. The death toll was not, however, caused by a pestilence but by the appalling lack of clothing. Miller, however, was a stickler for matters of hygiene, and the hospital Entry Book shows no evidence of smallpox or other contagious disease being prevalent.[66]

In a later issue the *Eastern Argus* printed a "burlesque" by an American officer, a prisoner on Melville Island, entitled the *Mandate of Miller*, which opens with these lines:

My Proclamation, wrote with labor,
If you can't read it ask your neighbour;
Ye Yankee prisoners, great and small,
Hear and tremble, at my word,
And if you don't, why then by G–!
You'd better wish, you'd not been born
Than treat me, or my word with scorn ...[67]

An extract from a prisoner's letter printed in the *Portland Gazette*, albeit a staunchly Federalist paper and greatly opposed to the war, stated that, "We fare very well as [it] respects our living: — If you have an opportunity, you will send to Mr. Miller, the Agent of the prisoners, and he will take care that I receive it; likewise any *money* you will send."[68] A comment on this extract by a Lieutenant Graham suggested that, "If Mr. Miller is such a wretch as he has been represented, is it likely that our prisoners would select him in preference to the American Agent, as the channel through which to obtain remittances, even of *money*?" The *Gazette* printed a further two extracts of letters from Melville Island: "There is no man of principle that can find fault with our treatment, as prisoners of war — There is Messrs [a list of names of prisoners followed] I believe to be all our friends that are here — they are all in good health, and wish to be remembered to their friends," and "We have plenty to eat, and Coffee twice a day."

In March 1814, the *Portland Gazette* printed a letter to the public from 11 prisoners of war on Melville Island, which went a long way toward righting the vilification heaped on Miller by a highly partisan press. These prisoners had heard that Miller had been attacked in a "scurrilous and malignant" manner respecting his treatment of prisoners of war and that he had behaved in a manner "cruel, fraudulent, and bordering on barbarity." The eleven claimed to speak with the approbation of the majority of the prisoners when they declared that they never experienced such treatment, but on the contrary they had "more clemency to our persons and attention to our necessaries" than was usual in other British establishments for prisoners of war. The letter concluded by stating "that these were the sentiments of the American Prisoners, which we attest to the Public, in justification of the character of a gentleman, & to prove the fallacy of such malign imposters as now gave occasion."[69]

Although this letter was dated 3 March 1814, prisoners on Melville Island apparently did not learn of it until sometime in the summer of that year. They formed a committee to prepare a reply, to what they called a "spurious publication." Their response appeared in the *Essex Register* in August, and it relied on declarations by prisoners who had been on Melville Island for periods between six and eighteen months. From the best information that the committee could obtain, they concluded that the letter of 3 March was drawn up by the head turnkey John Grant.[70] Their letter then described Miller's behaviour in the summer of 1813 when the prisoners refused to receive "stinking meat." He addressed them:

> *You shall not have an ounce of any other until you eat this, God damn you. When one of the prisoners answered that it would be the means of creating disease in the prison, he replied, "You may get sick and be damned; there is a hospital for you; & you may die & be damned — there is one hundred and fifty acres of land to bury you in, God damn you. I give my honor that every ounce of powder and shot on this island shall act against you if my orders are not complied with, God damn you." He then ordered the meat to be served out — the prisoners received it and threw it into the river [sic].*[71]

The committee's letter also provided another instance of Miller's supposed tyranny. Miller had mustered the prisoners and told them they had to assist in building a wall to enclose the prison. If they did not assist in building it, they would be shut up in the prison building for 20 hours out of 24. If anyone attempted to prevent those who were inclined to work from working, he would confine them to the black hole for 10 days and send them to England.

Charges of ill-treatment of American prisoners while they were at Quebec and enroute to Halifax appeared in the *New York Gazette*. In answering these charges Thomas Barclay commented that he was assured that if General Mason knew or even suspected of injustice to American prisoners he would have informed him. Mason had not done so.[72] Moreover, Barclay noted that the American agents in London, Quebec and Halifax had the best opportunity of knowing in what manner the prisoners under their care had been treated. He had not been informed that any of them had made complaints.

Benjamin Waterhouse's attitude toward Miller was equivocal. Even after Waterhouse realized that he and other prisoners selected by Miller — believing that they were being sent home — found themselves aboard a man-of-war in Halifax Harbour destined for Dartmoor, he remembered that, "However, it may be accounted for, we saw this man part from us with regret. It seemed to be losing an old acquaintance, while we were going we knew not where — to meet we knew not what." This ambivalence about "old Jimy square foot" seems to have been shared by a good many prisoners, who knew that Miller made the decision on whether they would be exchanged or sent to Dartmoor. In turn, Miller's superiors depended on him to run Melville Island in an orderly and efficient manner, for which he needed to retain the prisoners' co-operation, albeit grudgingly, given their circumstances. Benjamin Waterhouse probably summed up a general feeling when he wrote, "It is possible that we may not have made due allowance for Mr. Miller, the British agent, and we may have sometimes denounced him in terms of bitterness, when he did not deserve it. His general conduct, however, we could not mistake."

Miller had his standards of conduct. For example, he took the matter of breaking parole very seriously, as he demonstrated when three English prisoners in Boston did so. They escaped in a half-decked schooner-rigged boat and sailed it to Halifax. On arrival they were immediately confined on board a warship. Miller offered them to John Mitchell to be at his disposal. If he did see fit to send them back, Miller said that, "they should be made an example of, and turned before the mast on board a man of war."[73] The *Boston Gazette* commented that if the American government would show the same magnanimity it would be a serious warning to those who might be placed in a similar situation on both sides.

Whatever the charges of ill-treatment at Melville Island appearing in Republican newspapers, the Americans had no similar facility. They kept British prisoners in common gaols or makeshift prisons, often under dreadful conditions, and moved them around. Former British consuls residing in Atlantic seacoast towns were subject to all the regulations applicable to British subjects while they remained in the United States. Their major duty was to receive British prisoners of war from American marshals for placing on cartels destined for British ports. While American prisoners of war on Melville Island had Mitchell to intervene on their behalf, provide them with tobacco, clothing and other necessities, British agents had no such responsibilities, with the result that British prisoners of war were completely at the mercy of their guards and keepers.

While still at Salem a prisoner known only as T.D., a "plain jack-tar," sent a letter by a cartel to Halifax describing his ill-treatment as a prisoner of war. It exceeded the most outrageous charges of British cruelty appearing in the American press. Before printing T.D.'s letter the *Acadian Recorder* spoke with his fellow-sufferers who had arrived in the cartel, to ensure its authenticity.

T.D.'s narrative began with his capture at Fox Islands off the Maine coast. He was marched with three other prisoners 70 miles to Wiscasset, where they were told they would be put on a cartel, but found to their sorrow that they were headed to a dungeon. They were placed in a cell of darkness and despair, full of dung and dirt, for six weeks. At one time they were neglected by the keeper for so long that they were almost floating in their own excrement. Their sparse rations allowed for only a single meal a day. Finally, they were moved to a blockhouse, where 27 prisoners were closely confined in a room 10 by 18 feet. They were then moved to the Portland gaol, where they remained for two days, before being marched to Charlestown near Boston. They needed a broad axe to cut the bread they were given into edible pieces.

At Charlestown, they were told by "false tongues of these monsters" that they would be put aboard a cartel, but instead it was a prison ship. When they protested to the prison steward, who was skimming off the best of their beef ration for himself, he told them if ever they came to him with any more complaints, "he make us eat the Devil." They were again moved to a prison ship at Salem, where the salt beef given them stank so badly it could not be eaten, and many threw it overboard. When they refused to take any more for two days, they got none, and so were forced to take the beef offered. Their guards often beat them and threatened to kill them if they opened their mouths. When one prisoner sarcastically remarked that they had

Within weeks of the war's declaration, HMS Indian *captured off of St. Andrew's in the Bay of Fundy the privateer* Friendship *out of Salem. As a prize* Friendship *earned her captors £103.*

better hang them at once, an officer answered, "God D — d you, I hope I shall see you all hung yet — you deserve it every man of you." Their small prison ship, containing 250 men, leaked so badly that every time it rained they were almost afloat in their berths. No one was allowed to speak to them, nor could they obtain newspapers or news of any sort.

T.D. considered Americans:

… a lying, deceiving race, whose only delight is in tormenting and betraying their fellow-creatures. Like the cankerworm, they feed on the miseries of mankind. Let none of my countrymen ever trust, or depend on the Word or Honor of a Yankee: for truth they cannot speak…. If any of you are taken, run away if possible, if you love your liberty; or you may be caught as I was, and find a hell before you leave this world.[74]

CHAPTER 4
FROM BRUTAL RETALIATIONS TO PEACE

Retaliation and Counter Retaliation

Both Britain and the United States were prepared to retaliate when they believed the other had committed an unjustifiable act against prisoners, by using hostages as bargaining tools. The pattern of retaliation and counter retaliation began with the British capture of the sloop USS *Nautilus* in July 1812.[1] On her arrival at Halifax, six of the crew were found to be British subjects and were sent to England. The American government was aware of this action, and when USS *Constitution* brought HMS *Guerriere* into Boston 12 of her crew were imprisoned in retaliation for the six of the *Nautilus*. Although there was no doubt that the six men from the *Nautilus* were British subjects, sufficient proof could not be obtained for five of them to satisfy a court and jury in a trial. Accordingly, the British government released the five and sent them to the United States. The United States then released ten of the *Guerriere's* crew.

While American prisoners captured in the Battle of Queenston Heights, on 12 October 1812, were being shipped to Halifax, British officers reputedly mingled with the American captives and singled out those with a distinct Irish accent or who were otherwise considered to be British subjects.[2] Twenty-three were selected and sent to Britain for trial for bearing arms against the king.[3] Although the United States Congress gave President Madison authority to take retaliatory action, he did not do so until the following May, when he ordered the confinement of 23 British soldiers to be kept as hostages. On orders from the British government, Sir George Prevost, as commander-in-chief at Quebec, then placed 46 American officers and non-commissioned officers in close confinement, to be held as hostages for the safe keeping of the 23 British soldiers. In reaction, President Madison directed that all British commissioned

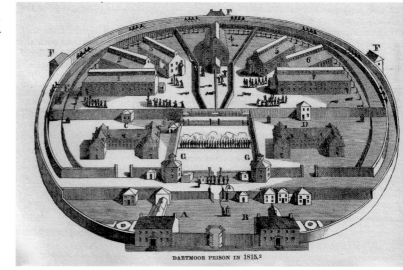

DARTMOOR PRISON IN 1815.[2]

This image of Dartmoor Prison appears as the front piece in copies of Benjamin Waterhouse's, A journal of a Young Man of Massachusetts late a surgeon on board a Privateer, *published in Boston in 1816.*

Robert Field painted this portrait of Sir George Prevost while he was lieutenant governor of Nova Scotia from 1808 until 1811 when he was appointed governor general of the Canadas.

officers of any rank in the states of Massachusetts, Kentucky and Ohio be placed in close confinement as a means of ensuring that the United States had sufficient numbers of hostages to match those being held by the British. Further retaliatory actions were taken as a result of the surrender of 59 Americans, claimed to be British subjects, captured at the Battle of Beaver Dam in June 1813.

Negotiations were underway to end retaliatory actions when, in September 1813, the Halifax authorities took 16 American prisoners (six officers from privateers and ten men from the *Chesapeake*) from Melville Island and placed them in the Halifax town gaol, in retaliation for the American confinement of eight British pris-

oners from the privateer *Decatur*.[4] On learning that several American prisoners of war were in the town gaol, Mitchell wrote Miller asking to be informed of the particular offence of each person or the reason for his incarceration.[5] He wanted to visit them either alone or in the company of Miller. He was especially concerned about one of them who had broken parole and who he believed was likely to be severely treated. Mitchell almost certainly never visited the town gaol or the prisoners, but he wrote John Mason with a graphic description of the presumed dungeon where the prisoners were being kept. Mason replied that in retaliation British prisoners of equivalent grade and number had been placed in dungeons "precisely" similar to those described by Mitchell.[6] However, according to the author of the Statement, published in the *Federal Republican* on 29 December 1813, the Mitchell report that had appeared in American newspapers was "wholly unfounded, with respect to the nature of the place [Halifax town gaol] in which the sixteen American prisoners were confined."[7]

As proof that Mitchell's representations to the United States government were incorrect, the Statement reported that Washington had received a description of the Halifax gaol in which 16 men had been confined, along with descriptions of the prison ship and Melville Island prison against which no complaint had been made. The author said that the severe treatment of the 16 British prisoners in Massachusetts, ten of whom were literally put into dungeons, was a consequence of Mitchell's erroneous report of the "wretched" conditions under which the Americans were being held.[8]

When Admiral Sir John Warren was informed, probably by Thomas Barclay, of Mitchell's unfounded report, he ordered the 16 prisoners to be returned to Melville Island or sent to Dartmouth to remove any further cause of

On Sunday the 6th of June the Shannon, *under the temporary command of Provo Wallace, a native Haligonian, sailed into Halifax Harbour towing the* Chesapeake *with 317 prisoners destined for Melville Island.*

complaint. Presumably, William Miller wrote the descriptions of the Halifax gaol and Melville Island sent to the American government through Barclay. The author of the Statement was correct that the British officers confined in retaliation were living in wretched conditions. The dungeons were seven feet by ten, on the gaol's ground floor, and were built of rough stone on wall, floor and ceiling. There were three loopholes, two or three inches wide, to admit a little light and air. What kept the prisoners alive in the winter was warm clothing provided by some charitable individuals.

They languished in these conditions, four to a dungeon, for three months. When news arrived that ten of the petty officers of the *Chesapeake* had been released, the ten British officers were finally removed from the dungeon.

American newspapers had regularly carried reports of the 16 American prisoners placed in the Halifax gaol in reputedly dreadful conditions. The *Salem Register,* when reporting on prisoners sent to Ipswich, Massachusetts, said that 100 English soldiers were to be detained in retaliation for those unaccountably selected from American prisoners at Halifax and sent to England. It sarcastically commented that, "We understand the war is expected shortly to be carried out by hangings ..."[9] Under the headline "Further British Outrages!" the *Eastern Argus* reported that a letter received from Halifax had said 101 seamen had been selected from Melville Island and sent to England.[10] The 16 who had been sent to the Halifax gaol had been confined to three cells and not allowed to see anyone. The unnamed letter writer had written to Miller, but the fact was that "he has no power."[11]

The *Portland Gazette* reported the names of the six officers confined at Halifax and stated that all American officers and others on parole had been confined to Dartmouth and that no communication with them was possible except by official permit.[12] Lieutenant George Budd, the senior captured officer of the *Chesapeake*, had written to Miller, apparently in protest, but his letter had been returned unopened with the notation that "no communication would be received from him." All communications were to be sent through Mitchell, as the American agent.[13] Moreover, it was understood there would be no further exchanges of prisoners until orders were received from the British government and the balance of prisoners due to the British had been paid.

In the midst of this brutal retaliation and counter retaliation, the Halifax authorities allowed some American prisoners to enjoy the advantages of the town by attending an entertainment at the Masonic Hall. Part of the entertainment was a celebration of the Battle of Martinique (presumably the battle fought between the British and French navies on 17 April 1780 off Martinique). A "beautiful transparency" was displayed and the patriotic song of the *Shannon* called for. When the lines, "Three cheers my brave fellows the proud *Chesapeake* has lowered her flag to the *Shannon*," were sung the American prisoners present rose as one and destroyed the transparency. They also attempted to destroy a pillar that could have brought down the building.[14] The theatre manager extricated the ladies present by ushering them across the stage into an adjoining room. The prisoners in question were probably officers of the *Chesapeake* on parole, who no doubt would have been once again confined to Dartmouth.

Some prisoners were put in the hold of the prison ship moored off Melville Island. Mitchell again erroneously reported to his government that these prisoners were constantly confined in the "Hole" of the prison ship from 2 o'clock in the afternoon until 10 o'clock the next day. In fact, they had never been placed in the "Hole" but lived between decks.[15] By January 1814, there were reportedly 92 Americans held in close confinement in Halifax in retaliation for 46 officers imprisoned by order of President Madison.[16]

In June 1814, John Mason sent two letters of instructions to John Mitchell on priorities for selecting prisoners for exchange. He also bypassed Mitchell, Lieutenant-Governor Sherbrooke and Admiral Warren and wrote directly to William Miller with a request for the seamen of USS *Wasp* to receive priority for exchange over all others, presumably because they were members of the United States Navy. Mitchell for a third time incorrectly informed

Mason when he stated that some of *Wasp*'s crew were in strict confinement, suspected of being British subjects. This had never been the case.[17] Mason told Mitchell that he was to make a return of all those put in dungeons and use all his power to have them sent home. Mason suggested that, as the Halifax depot was so full of prisoners, the British would be motivated by humanity to permit their release.[18]

The pattern of retaliation and counter retaliation was finally broken by implementation of a convention signed on 16 July 1814. According to the convention, all prisoners were to be exchanged with the exception of the 23 "Irish Traitors," 23 British soldiers initially held as hostages and the 46 Americans held at Halifax as hostages.[19] At Halifax exchanges by cartels were renewed and any hostages were likely included, if they had not already been sent to Dartmoor.

By the autumn of 1813 correspondence between John Mason and Thomas Barclay over the exchange of prisoners began to assume an acrimonious tone. On his appointment as agent, Barclay had insisted on living at an estate outside New York, which meant that correspondence with Mason took considerably more time than if he had resided in Washington. Mason now issued an order requiring Barclay to reside at a village outside Washington, and Barclay was living there when the British captured and burnt Washington in August 1814. Mason accused Barclay of attempting to communicate with the British forces and declined to hold any further correspondence with him. Barclay returned to New York and then sailed from there for England in October.[20]

When news of the United States' government decision and of Barclay's departure arrived at Halifax, Admiral Warren ordered John Mitchell to remove from Halifax within six days and not to visit the town or American prisoners at Melville Island again without special permission.

Since Mitchell's arrival Sherbrooke had been suspicious of him, and now he was emphatic that there "should be no American Agent of Mr. Mitchell's character" at Halifax.[21]

Mason wrote Mitchell that he had informed President Madison of Mitchell's removal order. The measure had come as a surprise and was seen as a response to the treatment meted out to Colonel Barclay.[22] Mason did not consider the two actions as being of the same kind. Only with difficulty and at a high rent was Mitchell able to obtain a house, named Sherwood, overlooking Bedford Basin. As well as being outside Halifax the house was eight miles from Melville Island, causing much more expense for him. He wrote Mason that, "I am here just five miles from Halifax and yet I appear to be isolated and enclosed in wood as if in the interior of Kentucky. I hear nothing of what is passing, all I can gather is from Halifax journals which you will find contain little intelligence."[23]

In place of Barclay the British appointed Gilbert Robertson, but he proved unacceptable to the American government. On his return to England, Robertson stopped at Halifax in November 1814, where he informed the authorities of the American government's refusal to accept him as Barclay's successor. The Halifax authorities concluded that the Americans were no longer interested in having a resident British agent. At the same time, Thomas Jeffery reported that Mitchell was sending information on smugglers to American customs officials. Mitchell was ordered to leave Halifax within six days, and he was strictly prohibited from entering Halifax until he was ready to embark.[24]

He was not allowed to appoint a replacement agent, but he was able to appoint two officers on parole who could visit the prisoners at Melville Island and provide them with articles necessary for their health and comfort. Mitchell's apparently nefarious actions resulted in an extraordinary letter to John Osborn in the *Acadian Recorder* by "Zeno," who paid for the letter to be printed as an advertisement.[25] After he was ordered to move out of Halifax, Mitchell had employed Osborn, a merchant, as his agent in Halifax.[26]

Of Mitchell, Zeno wrote, "that noxious planet never approaches Halifax without bringing plague and disgrace along with him" and that Mitchell advises his government "to grant him a few additional dollars to secure the secrets of the Cabinet of Halifax." Although Osborn was a British subject, Zeno accused him of being a firm supporter of the measures of President Madison and engaging in "deep designing Yankee tricks." Zeno had learned that Mitchell was about to depart and believed, incorrectly, that Osborn would become agent *pro temp*, which would give him an office well adapted to carry on his deceptions and conceal from investigation his correspondence with Mitchell while at Sherwood. Lieutenant-Governor Sherbrooke certainly had no use for Mitchell, but apparently did not associate any of his activities with Osborn, as earlier in September he had issued letters of marque and reprisal to Osborn for his schooner *Ann* to sail as a privateer.[27]

Mitchell arrived at New York with his family on 13 December. As of 20 November Mitchell informed the press that between 400 and 500 American prisoners had been sent to England. There remained upwards of 900 who were all well provided with food and lodgings and generally in excellent health. Of all the prisoners at Halifax no more than 30 were in the hospital.[28]

However, losses on bills of exchange drawn on the American government and the high cost of living in wartime Halifax had placed Mitchell in serious financial difficulties. General Mason had also reprimanded Mitchell for his failure to submit his accounts as required and this had caused further difficulties.[29] Mason had only honoured them to avoid any consequent disgrace to the United States. After the war Mitchell discovered that he was liable for the $5,000 he had drawn on John Osborn. He could not recover the amount from Osborn because the latter had absconded to the West Indies as a bankrupt. Osborn's own financial problems probably had their origin in the loss of his schooner *Ann*, shortly after Sherbrooke issued letters of marque for her to sail as a privateer. Zeno knew of the loss and commented that it "begins to show you in your full lustre."[30] Mitchell's private and public debts amounted to nearly $12,000. In 1824, he appealed to the United States Congress to relieve him of his outstanding debt due the United States. It is unknown whether his petition was successful. He died in 1830.

William Miller Replaced as Agent

The charges of ill-treatment of prisoners appearing in the American press were probably the chief factor in the Admiralty's decision on 16 November 1813 to appoint Miller as agent in Bermuda and for the agent there, Captain John Cochet, (pronounced "Cuchet") to replace Miller as agent at Halifax.[31] Cochet arrived in early May 1814, apparently with orders for Miller to proceed to the Bermuda Station.

Another factor that brought about Miller's removal may have been concern by the Transport Board that he had not been strictly following regulations. Shortly after taking over as agent, Cochet made it clear that he would grant no favour whatever to any person, but would conform to his instructions to the letter, implying that Miller had been responsible for unauthorized actions.[32] A possible example was Miller's taking of a French prisoner as his servant, then rewarding the man by discharging him and sending him to England so that he could return to his native country. For this the board reprimanded Miller, ordering him to never again repeat such an action.[33]

A Hundred Years of Peace *by Amédée Forrestier depicts the signing of the Treaty of Ghent on 24 December 1814 ending the war.*

Although the details are confusing, a further factor may have been the circumstances surrounding Miller's dismissal of an employee in his office. In February 1814, Miller had told Stephen Goddard that he would be dismissed, but could remain in Miller's office until the end of March. Miller accused him of asking captains of neutral ships for money. The ships in question could have been truly neutral or may have been American smugglers flying flags of neutral countries.[34] In a diatribe printed in the *Acadian Recorder* of 27 August, Goddard denied the charge and claimed that Miller had told him to take money for issuing certificates. He made other charges as well, including berating

Word of peace arrived in Halifax in March 1815. This watercolour of celebratory fireworks on Georges Island would have been seen in the sky by exuberant prisoners on Melville Island.

Miller for his conduct toward his servants, and for using that oft-repeated expression to the prisoners, "you may die and be damn'd the king has 150 acres to bury you."[35]

Whatever the cause or causes of Miller being replaced by Cochet, the decision gave Lieutenant-Governor Sir John Sherbrooke much concern. He commended Miller, while referring to the fears of a prisoner uprising during the winter of 1813-14, for the "zeal, activity and unremitting attention" that he had shown.[36] Miller had married Sarah Tucker in 1812. She was related to the prominent Halifax Blackadar family, so the Goddard affair would have had greater ramifications in Halifax for Miller than if he had not married into that family.[37] Miller remained in Halifax until at least late August because he did not conclude the sale of his house in Halifax's northern suburbs, near the Naval Hospital, until 22 August.

Miller left for Bermuda in the cartel *Matilda*, having charge of the prisoners to be exchanged. When the *Matilda* docked at Salem, Miller chose to visit the town and apparently made a favourable impression. The *Salem Gazette* commented that "Upon the whole, we have heard and seen so much of Mr. Miller, that we dare not consent to an unqualified charge, and must believe, upon the whole, in a trying situation, he will be found not to be altogether unworthy of the kind recollection of many of our worthy prisoners."[38] Miller might have used indiscreet language when supposedly provoked, but while in Salem the *Gazette* said "nothing was discovered unworthy of the best dispositions, and no letters which we have seen from our agents, or from our prisoners on parole, have discovered any apprehensions from anything which could arise from the purpose of Mr. Miller."

Peace

Representatives from Britain and the United States signed a Treaty of Peace and Amity at Ghent, Belgium on 24 December 1814, and ratification proceedings were completed by 17 February 1815. Article 3 of the treaty provided that, "All prisoners of war taken on either side, as well as by land as by sea shall be restored as soon as practicable after the ratifications of this treaty...."[39] When news of the Treaty of Ghent arrived at Halifax in March 1815, Cochet was ordered to release all the prisoners under his care and allow them to quit Halifax at their own expense or to leave on merchant vessels.[40] Ned Myers remembered the news:

> One evening in March 1815, we heard a great rejoicing in Halifax, and presently, a turnkey appeared on the walls and called out that England and America had made peace! We gave three cheers and passed the night happy enough. We had a bit of a row with the turnkeys about locking us in again, for we were fierce for liberty; but we were forced to submit for another night.[41]

Most prisoners returned in cartels sent by the Unites States. In direct contradiction to Mitchell's favourable report on the condition of prisoners at Halifax given to the New York papers, the *American Advocate* — as usual displaying its vociferously anti-British tone — reported that 350 prisoners, who had arrived at Salem on 23 March, agreed that, "their treatment in the Halifax prisons was brutal and barbarous in the extreme."[42] It charged the British with adopting an inhuman system, by which "to break down the spirits, the health and constitution of our unfortunate countrymen." As proof, it provided a figure of 50 deaths at Melville Island from 1 January to 12 March 1815. This matches the figure in the General Entry Book for the Melville Island hospital, so it must have been provided by Assistant Surgeon William MacDonald.[43]

However, the paper then claimed that a prisoner on Melville Island had told the editors that as many as 350 prisoners had died — a complete fabrication, because the total number of Americans who had died during captivity since the beginning of the war was only 188.

The *Advocate* also accused the prison authorities of providing bread sometimes containing such noxious substances as glass, pins, nails, tobacco, chips and dirt. In fact, this had happened on one occasion, which Mitchell had reported to John Mason. However, he was also able to report later with satisfaction that no more glass or dirt had been found in the bread. He hoped that the contractor would be more careful who he employed to do the baking, but "generally speaking the bread & beef are both Good."[44]

By mid-April there were only 120 prisoners remaining in Halifax.[45] In May, Cochet closed Melville Prison and delivered the remaining patients in its hospital to the Naval Hospital. By sending the prisoners home as rapidly as possible, the Halifax authorities avoided the kind of trouble that occurred at Dartmoor, which was housing some 5,000 Americans. Their imprisonment

A view of Deadman's Island looking north from the mainland, with Melville Island in the background.

continued even after both nations had ratified the treaty. The British assumed that the Americans would provide the necessary ships for the repatriation of the prisoners, but neither the American government nor its agent Reuben G. Beasley showed any particular haste.

Beasley, who had long been disliked by the prisoners for his neglect of their interests, now became an object of loathing. On 25 March a prisoner recorded that, "at Noon we had the Effigy of Mr. Beasley hung and then burnt for his kind attention to the American prisoners of war."[46] Matters became exceedingly tense. The upshot was an incident that the American prisoners called the "Dartmoor Massacre." On the orders of Captain Thomas Shortland troops fired into a gathering of prisoners on 9 April, reputedly because they feared an attempt at a mass escape. Seven prisoners died and 31 were wounded. The British authorities now acted. Those prisoners who could provide for themselves were allowed to leave immediately, while shipping was rapidly found for the remainder.

Although Melville Island was closed before the end of April, a considerable quantity of stores remained on Miller's charge. Around November 1815, the Transport Board ordered Miller to return to Halifax as its resident agent to discharge the whole establishment and then to return to England without delay."[47] Miller was back in Halifax by December 1815 as resident agent.[48] Commissioner Philip Wodehouse of the Halifax Dockyard advised the Transport Board that the stores should be sold at a public auction.[49] Under Miller's name, an advertisement appeared for a public auction to be held at Melville Island on 21 February.[50]

Included in the auction were such stores as 1,170 hammocks and other bedding, iron stoves, coal tubs, numerous items of clothing, hospital cradles and sentry boxes. Miller arranged for a party of men to attend on the day of the auction and the day after to carry the stores to the opposite shore for purchasers. Miller's instructions were emphatic: as soon as he had discharged his responsibilities relating to the stores he was immediately to return to England. When Miller did not return by August 1816, the Transport Board ordered his pay stopped because he had not obeyed orders.[51]

Miller's return to England may have been delayed by a case before the Nova Scotia Supreme Court in which he was the plaintiff. Just before his departure for Bermuda, Miller had sworn out a deposition against Thomas Haigh Mason, a Halifax merchant, stating that Mason was indebted to him for £220 for principal, interest and damages for a bill of exchange that had been protested in London.[52] The debt related to charges for the brig *Telus* of the transport service. While Miller was in Bermuda his counsel, Simon Bradstreet Robie, had kept the case alive. On Miller's return to Halifax, Mason's counsel demanded that unless the case proceeded to trial — two years having elapsed — he would move for nonsuit (stoppage of a suit by a judge when the plaintiff fails to make out a legal case or bring sufficient evidence). At the Easter term of the Supreme Court in *Miller versus Mason* the verdict was "nonsuit." The last reference in the case file is a document dated 29 July, so Miller may still have been in Halifax at that date, but he did return to England sometime in 1816.[53] He presumably provided acceptable explanations for whatever concerns the Transport Board might have had about his conduct, as he was placed on half pay and given a pension for his 33 years of arduous service (he had obtained his lieutenancy in 1780).[54]

Deadman's Island

At the time of the establishment of Melville Island Prison, the small hill to its south, called Target Hill, had been used by naval ships for gunnery practice. In the nineteenth century it would become known as Deadman's Island. The first references to Target Hill being used for the burial of those who died while confined to Melville Island Prison comes from the privateer Benjamin Palmer's journal. On 26 May 1814 he noted, "Two persons have been taken to Target Hill this week," and on 4 June 1814, "… four Prisoners caried to Target Hill this morning a place where they bury the Dead."[55] Although not composed by Palmer, his *Journal* has some bitter doggerel, eight lines of which read:

> *Go view the graves which prisoners fill*
> *Go count them on the rising hill*
> *No monumental marble shows*

An aerial view of Melville Island and Deadman's Island.

> *Whose silent dust does there repose —*
> *Save that the papal cross is plac'd*
> *Next to the graves where papest [papists]*
> *rest*
> *All sleep unknown; their bodies not*
> *By all, save distant friends forgot.*[56]

Palmer's reference to what must have been wooden crosses placed on Roman Catholic graves provides contemporary evidence that French prisoners of war were buried on Deadman's Island. The Melville Island Prisoner Entry and Hospital Books recorded 261 deaths from such causes as fever, dysentery, smallpox and typhus from 17 August 1803 until 30 March 1815 when the prison closed. When François Bourneuf came to Halifax as a French prisoner of war in 1809, he first went to the Naval Hospital in the dockyard with the other wounded before being sent to Melville Island. Burial records for this hospital exist and prisoners who died while at the Naval Hospital would have been buried in its burial ground.[57]

Of the 1,535 French prisoners confined at one

time or another on Melville Island from 1803 until 1813, when Napoleon was forced into exile on the Island of Elba, 56 died.[58] Another nine Spanish prisoners (Spain was at the time France's ally) died between 22 August and 6 October 1805. After Napoleon returned from his exile in March 1815, more French prisoners arrived, and of these ten died. Thus, 66 French prisoners and nine Spaniards are recorded as having died from 17 August 1803 to 2 August 1814 while in Melville Prison. Most, if not all, of them would have been buried on Deadman's Island.

The first American death was recorded on 10 August 1812 and the last on 30 March 1815. Of 8,148 Americans imprisoned on Melville Island, 188 died while there and would have been buried on Target Hill.[59] Another seven died while in the Naval Hospital in Halifax and, like the French, would have been buried in its burial ground. In John Mitchell's papers there is a receipt for coffins for seamen from the Naval Hospital, and there is no reason why he should not have provided coffins for prisoners who died while on Melville Island.

CHAPTER 5

THE PARADOX OF MELVILLE ISLAND PRISON

In neither the Seven Years War nor the American War of Independence did Halifax serve as even a temporary staging location for prisoners of war. After the war with Revolutionary France began in 1793, French prisoners taken in the capture of St. Pierre and Miquelon, and others taken at sea, were brought to Halifax, but at the first opportunity they were sent to England. Still, the authorities at Halifax had to make what they considered temporary arrangements for French prisoners such as the purchase of a prison ship and allowing them to live in the town. The choice of Kavanagh's Island resulted not from a deliberate decision, but from the necessity of finding accommodation for French sick a sufficient distance from Halifax to satisfy a populace that feared the prisoners were carrying a malignant fever. When other prisoners residing in the town became unruly they were sent to Kavanagh's Island, where they were confined to a prison ship moored off the island and guarded by a small garrison. With the signing of the Treaty of Amiens in March 1801, all French prisoners were sent to France and the Kavanagh Island establishment was completely closed down.

When war broke out again in 1803 and French prisoners taken at sea were brought to Halifax, the immediate reaction was to send them to Britain. However, the prisoners needed to be accommodated. Vice Admiral Sir Andrew

Mitchell's solution was to lease Kavanagh's Island for a year. Meanwhile, the Admiralty had concluded that a full prisoner-of-war establishment at Halifax had become necessary and authorized the purchase of Kavanagh's Island. This was done and it was renamed Melville Island. As a result of wars in the eighteenth century, Britain had established war prisons under the Admiralty's Transport Board, with their own establishments and regulations for holding large numbers of prisoners of war. Melville Island became part of an established system of war prisons and prison ships with capacity to house thousands of prisoners. When faced with finding suitable accommodation, especially during the winter months, Vice Admiral Sir Andrew Mitchell ordered the construction of a wooden prison building, which was completed by September 1805, thus creating a permanent facility for holding prisoners of war.

There were to be no exchanges for French prisoners of war at Halifax, so their numbers kept increasing, reaching more than 1,500. From the arrival of the first French prisoners, the Halifax authorities had allowed them to find work in Halifax and outside the town, while still nominally on the prisoner roll for Melville Island. In addition, officers were place on parole and resided across the harbour at Dartmouth and Preston. Although the authorities placed greater restrictions on prisoners as escapes increased, the

policy remained generally lenient.

After the United States declared war in June 1812, American prisoners taken at sea began arriving at Halifax. They were treated, initially, with the same leniency as the French. Nearly all were privateers or merchant seamen, both of whom were treated as prisoners of war. As their numbers dramatically mounted and resentment intensified at the privateers' "depredations," there was a definite hardening of attitude. Vice Admiral Herbert Sawyer demonstrated this when he told the Admiralty that he had no intention of exchanging those taken as privateers. Although the Admiralty's instructions were to treat privateers as legitimate prisoners of war, at Halifax the unstated policy was to give them the lowest priority for exchanges and to ship them, when transport was available, to England and the

dreaded Dartmoor. A crucial reason for William Miller and the admirals on station refusing to allow the American agent, John Mitchell, any influence over the makeup of lists of prisoners at Melville Island for exchange was to keep privateers off the lists.

Initially, the Halifax authorities were prepared to send American prisoners home in cartels without requiring British prisoners to be sent to Halifax. Once the Halifax Agreement was signed in November 1812, the British began insisting that a balance be maintained for prisoner exchanges. This posed a serious problem for the Americans because the balance was almost always against them. The appointment of John Mason as commissary general for prisoners and Thomas Barclay as British agent in the United States did bring more order to arranging

Above: This view of south-east Boston in 1801 was published in England, which explains the numerous merchant vessels flying the Union Jack. President Jefferson's Embargo Act of 1807 would have drastic consequences for such New England ports as Boston. Left: Within weeks of the declaration of war by the United States in June 1812, a number of privateer captains thought of joining forces to seize St. Andrews, New Brunswick, but nothing came of the plan.

exchanges. But the lack of a permanent prison establishment like Melville Island on the eastern seaboard meant the arrangements for prison exchanges remained an *ad hoc* system at best on the American side. The result was long delays in arranging and obtaining approval for cartel sailings — to the great detriment especially of American prisoners of war confined at Melville Island.

Such delays turned into a virtual paralysis for arranging exchanges in the autumn of 1813, just at the time when Sir George Prevost began sending large numbers of captured American soldiers to Halifax. When the prison population exceeded 1,500, this caused major overcrowding. Where hammocks had previously been arranged in three tiers, they were now in four. This overcrowding caused justifiable fears of serious prisoner disturbances, if not attempts at mass escapes. Lieutenant-Governor Sherbrooke's request for more troops was refused, as was his recommendation to send prisoners to Pictou or Louisbourg. As winter approached, the lack of clothing for hundreds of prisoners reached crisis proportions.

Although William Miller continually warned John Mitchell of the approaching crisis, Mitchell failed or was unable to act. In the end Miller obtained the authority to provide hundreds of clothing items for the prisoners and averted what could have been a dreadful death toll throughout the winter. Sherbrooke credited Miller for getting Melville Island through the winter without any major breakdown in prison administration. In the spring of 1814 the British policy became to ship as many prisoners as possible to Dartmoor, and this policy was maintained until the end of the war. There was little the Americans could do when, in the final months of the war, the prison balance stood 3,000 against them.

Although it is generally believed that privateers made up most of the prisoners on Melville

Island, this was not the case. Of the 8,148 prisoners listed in the Entry Book,

Prisoner Category	Number
Privateers	3542
Merchant Seamen	2487
USS Army	1456
USS Navy	656

privateers accounted for slightly more than one-third, as shown in the table above.

Of the 92 privateer vessels captured that had their crews imprisoned on Melville Island, the home ports of 81 can be identified. Twenty-seven sailed out of Salem and eleven out of Boston. New York and Portsmouth were the home ports to eight privateers each and the remaining ports were Baltimore (six), Marblehead (three), Charleston (three), Kennebunk (one) and Hallowell (one).

The whole issue of the reputed ill-treatment of Melville Island prisoners is fraught with difficulties because of the varied nature of records and the question of how much significance should be given to each of them. There are personal narratives, prisoner letters to John Mitchell, prisoners' letters and numerous reports appearing in newspapers, official correspondence relating to prisoners of war and the correspondence found in John Mitchell's papers. Of the three personal narratives — those of Benjamin Waterhouse, Benjamin Palmer and Ned Myers — only that of Waterhouse makes reference to what might be described as ill-treatment. Although Waterhouse was disparaging of Miller's harangues from his rostrum at the head

of the stairs of the prison building, his single references are to Miller "cruelly" harassing the prisoners by his custom of mustering and parading them in the severest cold, even in snow storms, and keeping them outside in bad weather while the prison floors were washed, until they dried. Charges of cruelty by Miller that appeared in newspapers were in fact not related to specific accusations of any acts of deliberate cruelty, but to his harangues, especially his "the King has one hundred and fifty Acres of land appropriated to bury you in."

References to cruelty in the Mitchell Papers nearly all concerned prisoners treated as hostages during the period of retaliation and counter retaliation. On three different occasions Mitchell misled his government on what was happening to prisoners in Halifax, either deliberately or because he failed to determine the true facts before sending his reports of cruelty. The order to confine British officers in the Ipswich

A view of Salem Harbor in the early 19th century.

gaol's dungeon, where they were to remain for three months in wretched conditions, was given as a result of Mitchell's erroneous report. Except for this period, in all the letters from prisoners to John Mitchell, there is not a single one that even hints at cruel behaviour. Both sides cast prisoners who were caught escaping into black holes and dungeons. When it came to the use of the lash (prohibited under both cartels), this punishment was administered by the prisoners themselves after a trial conducted by them. It was no different from punishments used to maintain discipline in the armies and navies of the day.

If charges of sadistic cruelty could be laid, they would be against the ill-treatment suffered by the British officers in Ipswich gaol, by Joseph Barss in the Portsmouth gaol and by T.D. and his brother prisoners at the hands of American keepers and guards. These British prisoners had no redress, unlike the Americans at Melville Island who could protest to Mitchell. The most telling evidence that charges of cruel behaviour on Melville Island had little substance is borne out by the lack of such charges to be found in the correspondence between John Mason and Thomas Barclay, where one would expect to find it. As Anthony Deitz in his PhD thesis, *The Prisoner of War in the United States during the War of 1812*, points out, "The correspondence between the two principal agents reveals no such charges."[1]

There could not have been two characters more different — in personality and experience — than William Miller and John Mitchell. Yet these two individuals in many ways controlled the fate of those who had the ill fortune to become prisoners of war at Melville Island. After more than 30 years of naval service Miller was determined to run a tight ship and had to do so under very demanding conditions. As much as the prisoners detested Miller and the turnkeys, they knew that decisions about whether they would be sent home or to Dartmoor largely rested with Miller. At the same time Miller needed a prison population that would accept his rule to the degree necessary to run the prison in an orderly and efficient manner, as expected by his superiors. Theirs was a tense, resentful and ambivalent relationship, but it could not have been otherwise under the circumstances.

In describing John Mitchell as "an elderly gentleman," the prisoners accurately portrayed their feelings about him. Distrusted by the Halifax

Baltimore was home port to at least a dozen or so privateers, but of those captured only six were brought to Halifax. Most notably, however, was the Rolla, *8 guns and a crew of 95, for which her purchasers paid £88 and sent her to sea again as a Nova Scotian privateer. Another was the* Huzzar, *with a crew of 97, which earned her captors of HMS Saturn £106.*

authorities and never able to select prisoners for exchange, he lapsed into providing such items as tobacco and newspapers. His preference was for the society of the officers residing in the upper storey. Benjamin Waterhouse had perhaps a harsher opinion of Mitchell than he did of Miller. Waterhouse felt strongly that Mitchell had not made sufficient effort "to relieve the wants of our suffering companions."[2] Although Mitchell might be a very good man, Waterhouse believed he should never have been employed in a station that required "high health and activity" and he blamed the American government for its poor choice in appointing Mitchell.

Mitchell, however, did not suffer the humilia-tion of his counterpart in England, Reuben Beasley, who American prisoners in Dartmoor burnt in effigy because of his neglect of them.

There is no way of reconciling Mitchell's state-ment to the New York press on his return from Nova Scotia in December 1814, in which he said that the remaining prisoners at Melville Island were "all well furnished with food and lodgings, and are generally in excellent health," with a report in the *Eastern Argus* stating that prisoners arriving back after the declaration of peace all agreed that, "their treatment in the Halifax pris-ons was brutal and barbarous in the extreme."

Such is the underlying paradox of the Melville Island Prison story.

EPILOGUE
FROM 1815 TO THE PRESENT DAY

Chesapeake Blacks: April 1815 – May 1816

Hardly had Melville Island Prison been closed than it had to be reopened to care for the expected arrival of former black slaves, who had sought freedom by fleeing to British warships blockading Chesapeake Bay on the American eastern seaboard. About 1,200 former slaves had already come to Nova Scotia, but the number of those fleeing increased after Admiral Sir Alexander Cochrane issued a proclamation in April 1814, promising every encouragement for them to become free settlers in North America.

In the expectation that as many as 2,000 would shortly be arriving for settlement in Nova Scotia and New Brunswick, the Nova Scotia government appointed Thomas Jeffery, Collector of Customs, to make arrangements. He chose Melville Island as the depot where the black refugees would be provided with rations, clothing and medical care. From April to July 1815, 727 Chesapeake blacks, as they would be called, were sent to Melville Island, where an average of 39 a day were admitted to the former prison hospital.[1] In succeeding months more continued to arrive and be sent to Melville Island, where many received care in the hospital. Before the government closed the depot and the hospital in June 1816, out of the hundreds who had been cared for in the hospital since April 1815, at least 104 had died and were presumably buried on Deadman's Island. Since many died of smallpox and typhus, it is highly unlikely they would have been transferred elsewhere for burial.

Quarantine Station and Hospital for Irish Immigrants: June – October 1847

Melville Island was first used as a quarantine station for a short period in 1818.

By 1829, when Thomas Chandler Haliburton published his *Historical and Statistical Account of Nova Scotia* the buildings were very run down. He described Melville Island as situated in the centre of a little cove, the former abode of unfortunate prisoners of war:

> There are about ten buildings upon it, which, together with a garden, nearly cover its surface. The principal one is the prison, a long wooden house, two stories in height, whose grated windows bespeak the use to which it has been applied. All the buildings are in a state of neglect and decay ...[2]

The island was again used as a quarantine station for short periods in 1831 and 1846, and also for the 1,200 Irish who arrived in Halifax, mostly in May and June 1847, after fleeing from the great potato famine.[3] Many were suffering from smallpox and typhus. The Board of Health ordered all incoming Irish to be quarantined on

Melville Island. Neither the two doctors, James Hume and Matthew Hoffman, nor the matron, Nurse Mary Fitzgerald, were allowed off the island. After the hospital closed in early October, the Board of Health reported that 203 patients had been admitted to the fever hospital, 30 had died, 163 had been discharged as cured, and ten elderly patients transferred to the Poor Asylum.[4] Like the Chesapeake blacks, the 30 Irish immigrants who died while quarantined on Melville Island in 1847 were presumably buried on Deadman's Island.

The Foreign Legion: May 1855

In an attempt to recruit men for the Crimean War, the British government passed an act in 1855, entitled the Foreign Enlistment Act, which provided for the recruitment of foreigners. Attempts to recruit in the United States ran into the difficulty of American neutrality in the war between Great Britain, France and Turkey against Russia, which precluded recruiting in that country. However, a plan was concocted, largely by Joseph Howe, whereby men would be engaged for employment on railway construction in Nova Scotia — a deception, as they were really being recruited as part of a Foreign Legion to serve in the Crimea. When the recruits arrived in Nova Scotia, they were accommodated at Melville Island, which also served as a processing depot before their departure to England. A nominal roll dated 31 May 1855, giving name, rank and date of enlistment, listed 158 names.[5] However, after the deception became public knowledge, the scheme collapsed. In June, the British government abandoned the project and Joseph Howe returned home to Halifax.[6]

British Army Military Prison: 1856–1909

By the 1850s, it was no longer practical to keep military prisoners at the Halifax Citadel. An obvious alternative was Melville Island. After considerable negotiation, transfer of the island and buildings from the Admiralty to the War Department was completed in 1856, and 70 prisoners were moved to the old wooden prison building.[7] When the British Army took over Melville Island the only two buildings standing were the old wooden prison and the officers' quarters, and they were both unoccupied. A plan drafted in 1860 showed, in addition to these two buildings, a stable, shed, cookhouse, wash house and well. There were also two wells on the mainland and a guardhouse immediately across the bridge joining the island to the mainland. In either 1884 or 1905 (the correct date is not at all clear), a new stone building with 34 cells was erected adjoining the old wooden prison.[8] Melville Island was located near two quarries, one ironstone and the other granite, and so much of the prisoners' time was occupied by breaking stone.

A miniature of Doctor Matthew Hoffman. Melville Island was used as quarantine station for the 1,200 Irish who arrived in Halifax, after fleeing from the great potato famine. All were sent to Melville Island. Neither the two doctors, James Hume and Matthew Hoffman, nor the matron, Nurse Mary Fitzgerald, were allowed off the island while the quarantine order was in effect.

This view of Melville Island, entitled Barracks of the Foreign Legion, *appeared in the* Illustrated London News *of May 19, 1855.*

As part of the arrangements to transfer responsibility for the defence of Halifax from the British garrison to Canada, the Canadian Permanent Force took over the prison in December 1905. It then housed three prisoners. In 1907 the War Department transferred Melville Island, along with other military property, to the Dominion of Canada.

Purchase by Charles Longley

Around 1850, as a small boy, W.R. Geldert remembered visiting Deadman's Island and seeing a number of shallow graves, which had been uncovered by a heavy storm, exposing human skeletons.[9] By the turn of the twentieth century, Melville Cove had become a popular location for boaters.

Although the Admiralty had handed over Melville Island to the War Office in 1857, it still retained possession of property on the mainland and also Deadman's Island. In August 1907, Charles Longley, a Halifax ship and freight broker, purchased much of the original 1752 grant, including Deadman's Island, from the Admiralty for £863 sterling. Longley turned the island into a park, called Melville Park. On the Island's tip he built a dance hall, served by a ferry that he ran from the bottom of Jubilee Road on the Halifax side of the Northwest Arm and across from Deadman's. As well as the dance hall, Longley erected his own house, Pinehaven, on the island.[10]

John Dixon's Grave Site

When subdividing Deadman's into lots, Charles Longley apparently moved the evidence of the lone marked grave on the island, that of one

John Dixon, which today cannot be located. At some point a picture was taken of the gravesite and the wooden memorial marker was later found and deposited in the Nova Scotia Museum. The wording on the marker reads:

Sacred to the Memory
of
John Dixon
of Sydney, K[C].B.
who died on the
6th of August 1817.
Aged 21 Years
Erected by the
VIII King's Foot
Renewed by 1st Royal
Berkshire Regiment, 1895

Curator Harry Piers of the Nova Scotia Museum determined that John Dixon was a Sydney, Cape Breton mariner, who had met his death in 1847 on the Northwest Arm and been buried on Deadman's. The date on the marker of 1817 was a mistake for 1847. Soldiers, reputedly of the VIII King's Foot, placed a wooden grave marker at the head of Dixon's grave. However, the VIII King's Foot never served in the Nova Scotia command at this period, although the VII King's Foot arrived from Barbados on 31 March 1848 and left for England on 29 May 1850. Members of the VII Foot must have found Dixon's grave already marked. At some point before their departure in 1850, the regiment replaced whatever marker was then in place. In 1895, the 1st Royal Berkshire Regiment renewed the marker. At that point, a mistake may have been made by carving VIII for VII and thus confusing the two regiments.

In 1908 John Regan, in his *Sketches of the Northwest Arm*, repeated a story that Dixon had been a young soldier and that he and a colonel's daughter had fallen in love. When their attach-ment became known, the colonel had Dixon committed to Melville Island military prison on a trumped-up charge where the lad committed suicide by drowning.[11] In fact, the story was a complete fabrication by a local newspaperman, designed solely to give a touch of romance to the lone grave.[12]

First World War to the Armdale Yacht Club: 1914–1947

When the First World War broke out, as many as 139 German and Austro-Hungarian reservists were removed from homeward bound vessels or captured at sea and interned on Melville Island for varying periods of time.[13] After the war many of the buildings were torn down, though not the wooden prison, which however burned down in 1935. Following the Second World War, there was much interest in Melville Island by the Armdale Yacht Club as a site for the club. In 1947, the Department of National Defence leased the island to the club for recreational purposes on a year-to-year basis. In 1956, the club negotiated a 99-year lease with National Defence.[14]

Halifax Regional Municipality Purchases Deadman's Island

Aside from Longley's dance hall and two houses there is no record of other structures on Deadman's Island. For most of the twentieth century, the island's chief use was for casual recreational activities, and from time to time, human remains were discovered on the shores of Deadman's Island. An archaeological survey was carried out in 1998 when residential development was contemplated, and it identified possible historical burial sites. However, no further archaeological work was carried out because in 2000 the Halifax Regional Municipality purchased the island to ensure preservation of its national and international historic significance.[15]

A Commemorative Memorial for Deadman's Island

Much of the credit for taking action to protect the site of Deadman's Island rests with the Northwest Arm Heritage Association and the Society of the War of 1812 in the state of Wisconsin. The discovery of the unmarked graves of Americans who had died while prisoners of war on Melville Island became a matter of interest in the United States, and the Society of the War of 1812 proposed that a memorial be erected on Deadman's Island. The Ohio Sons of the American Revolution, the Military Order of Foreign Wars of the United States and the American Legion supported this effort.

In Canada, the Royal Canadian Legion took up the cause. A Committee of the Halifax Regional Municipal Council was struck to advise on means to support the American interest to erect a memorial. The United States Department of Veteran Affairs, through its Memorial Programs Service, agreed to supply a Group Memorial monument. At a service on 30 May 2005 — Memorial Day in the United States — a commemorative ceremony was held on Deadman's Island for the unveiling of the Memorial, inscribed with the names of 195 Americans who died while prisoners of war in Halifax, of whom 188 were buried on Deadman's Island.

After American Service families laid flowers in respect of fallen American personnel, each represented by an American flag, piper Jeremy Blackburn played the "Last Lament of the Unknown Soldier."

ENDNOTES

CHAPTER 1

1. Land Grants, RG20, Series A, Bk. 2, p. 30, Nova Scotia Archives and Records Management (hereafter NSARM).

2. *Nova-Scotia Gazette* (Halifax), 27 February 1781.

3. Deeds, Halifax County, RG47, 8 January 1782, vol. 18, p. 1,000, NSARM.

4. Brian Cuthbertson, *The Loyalist Governor: Biography of Sir John Wentworth* (Halifax: Petheric Press, 1983), pp. 62-63.

5. Wentworth to Henry Dundas, 27 August 1793, CO217/64, f. 256, National Archives, London (hereafter NA).

6. *Royal Gazette and Nova Scotia Advertiser* (Halifax), 3 December 1793.

7. Copy of warrant appointing Mr. John Halliburton principal surgeon, 28 August 1794, Admiralty (hereafter ADM) 1/492, f. 424, NA.

8. John Halliburton to Admiral Robert Murray, 30 August 1794, ADM 1/492, f. 434, NA.

9. *Ibid.* For the use of Kavanagh's Island as a prison hospital, see Allan E. Marble, *Surgeons, Smallpox and the Poor: A History of Medicine and Social Conditions in Nova Scotia, 1749-1799* (Montreal& Kingston: McGill-Queen's University Press, 1993), p. 155. See also Iris Shea and Heather Watts, *Deadman's: Melville Island and Its Burial Ground* (Halifax: Glen Margaret Publishing, 2005), p. 14 (hereafter *Deadman's*) and J.P. LeBlanc, *A Detailed History of Armdale Yacht Club* (www.armdaleyachtclub.ns.ca).

10. ADM 1/492, f. 470, NA.

11. Admiral Robert Murray to Daniel Lyman, 28 August 1794, ADM 1/492, f. 424, NA.

12. Admiral Robert Murray to John Halliburton, 4 June 1795, ADM 1/493, f. 190, NA.

13. Thomas Beamish Akins, "History of Halifax," *Collections of the Nova Scotia Historical Society*, vol. 8 (1895), p. 110.

14. Admiral Robert Murray to Phineas Bond, 4 August 1795, ADM 1/493, f. 205, NA.

15. *Ibid.*

16. For the appointment of agents, arrangements relating to prisoners, rations, bedding and rules to be observed by them, see Thomas James Walker, *The Depot for Prisoners of War at Norman Cross Huntingdonshire, 1796 to 1816* (London: Constable & Company, 1915), pp. 39-66.

17. Gavin Daly, "Napoleon's Lost Legions: French Prisoners of War in Britain, 1803-1814," *Journal of the Historical Association*, vol. 89 (July 2004), p. 365.

18. Transport Board to John Beckwith, 2 June 1802, ADM 98/286, p. 11, NA.

19. General Entry Book of Soldier Prisoners of War, ADM103/170, NA.

20. General Orders, No. 1, 23 August 1803, MG12, Headquarters Office Papers for Nova Scotia 1783-1907, vol. 4, NSARM. See also Major H. Meredith Logan, "Melville Island: The Military Prison of Halifax," *Journal of the Royal United Services Institute*, vol. 6 (1933), pp. 12-34.

21. Transport Board to Captain Robert Murray, RN, 2 September 1803, ADM 98/286, p. 26, NA.

22. The Notice of Sale of Kavanagh's Island as it appeared in the *Royal Gazette*, 31 May 1804 is reproduced as Appendix I in *Deadman's*, p. 68. Deeds, Halifax County, RG47, 17 August 1804, Bk. 36, p. 314, NSARM. Kavanagh certainly obtained a good price for the land he had originally purchased for £65, though the extensive buildings he had erected had greatly increased its value. In 1796 Kavanagh had been in such financial difficulties that he had mortgaged all his properties, including his town house, for £1700. He had, however, gained his release from the mortgage three years later. See Deeds, Halifax County, RG47, indenture, 13 November 1796, Bk. 33, p. 324, NSARM. The buildings listed in the auction notice consisted of two large houses or prisons "which have contained 200 persons," two cookhouses, a dwelling house, a barracks for 25 to 30 persons, a servant's house and a guard house.

23. Transport Board to Captain John MacKellar, 5 September 1805, ADM 98/286, pp. 219-21, NA.

24. *Ibid.*

25. *Ibid.*

26. For William Hughes as a master builder, see Maud Rosinski, *Architects of Nova Scotia: A Biographical Dictionary 1605-1950* (Halifax: Department of Municipal Affairs, 1994), p. 43.

27. For the construction of Norman Cross Prison, see Thomas James Walker, *The Depot for Prisoners of War at Norman Cross Huntingdonshire, 1796 to 1816*, pp. 18-24.

28. Transport Board to Captain John MacKellar, 2 August 1804, ADM 98/286, p. 134. The contract for "soft bread" went to William Blake.

29. Standard issue of prisoner clothing in Britain was a yellow suit, grey or yellow cap, a yellow jacket, a red waistcoat and yellow trousers. See Thomas James Walker, *The Depot for Prisoners of War at Norman Cross Huntingdonshire, 1796 to 1816*, p. 73.

30. *Royal Gazette* (Halifax), 16 February 1808.

31. Much of the information on French prisoners of war on Melville Island comes from François Lambert Bourneuf's autobiography, edited and translated by J. Alphonse Deveau, *Diary of a Frenchman: François Lambert Bourneuf's Adventures from France to Acadia, 1787-1871* (Halifax: Nimbus Publishing, 1990).

32. Thomas Beamish Akins, History of Halifax, *Collections of the Nova Scotia Historical Society*, vol. 8 (1895), pp. 156-57.

33. Major H. Meredith Logan, "Melville Island: The Military Prison of Halifax," *Journal of the Royal United Services Institute*, vol. 6 (1933), p. 14.

34. For this incident, see Wentworth to Earl of Camden, 21 July 1805, CO217/80, f. 31, NA. See also Dianne Marshall "Murder on Melville Island," Novascotian section, Halifax *Sunday Herald*, 12 June 2005, pp. 3-4.

35. Wentworth to Mitchell, 5 May 1805, RG1, vol. 54, pp. 7-8, NSARM.

36. Keith Mercer, "Sailors and Citizens: Press Gangs and Naval-Civilian Relations in Nova Scotia, 1756-1815," *Journal of the Royal Nova Scotia Historical Society*, vol. 10 (2007), pp. 102-03.

37. At Norman Cross Prison violent deaths came before a coroner's jury. Thomas James Walker, *The Depot for Prisoners of War at Norman Cross Huntingdonshire, 1796 to 1816*, pp. 149-50. Similarly at Dartmoor, where violent deaths from suicide, duel or murder were so frequent that the district coroner called for an increased fee for jurors. Francis Abell, *Prisoners of War in Britain 1756 to 1815: A Record of their Lives, their Romance and their Sufferings* (London: Humphrey Milford, 1914), p. 251 (hereafter *Prisoners of War in Britain 1756 to 1815*).

38. Wentworth to Mitchell, 5 May 1805, RG1, vol. 54, p. 8, NSARM.

39. Report of the Case of Pierre Poulin..., attached to Wentworth to Earl of Camden, 21 July 1805, CO217/80, ff. 31-32 and ff. 33-34, NA.

40. Secretary of State Lord Castlereagh to Wentworth, 5 September 1805, RG1, vol. 60, doc. 74, NSARM.

41. Beamish Murdoch, *History of Nova Scotia*, vol. III, p. 244. Murdoch was a small boy at the time and would have known of the

events surrounding the public hanging. Neither Murdoch nor T.B. Akins, when describing the almost idyllic life of the French prisoners, mention the hanging, though both would have known of it in detail.

42. *Diary of a Frenchman*, p. 50.

43. *Ibid*.

44. A.J. Rhodes, *Dartmoor Prison: A Record of 126 Years of Prisoner of War and Convict Life, 1806-1932* (London: John Lane and Bodley Head Limited), pp. 26 and 37.

45. For a list of French prisoners who escaped, see *Deadman's*, pp. 69-72.

46. *Royal Gazette* (Halifax), 2 May 1809.

47. *Royal Gazette* (Halifax), 4 July 1805, and *Weekly Chronicle*, 12 November 1813.

48. *Weekly Chronicle* (Halifax), 25 April 1813.

49. Transport Board to Captain J. MacKellar, 7 May 1807, ADM 98/286, NA.

50. Transport Board to MacKellar, 8 August 1806, ADM 98/286, pp. 83-86, NA.

51. *Diary of a Frenchman*, pp. 47-68.

52. *Deadman's*, pp. 75-76.

53. Notice in the *Weekly Chronicle* (Halifax), 29 July 1808, for "building a house on Melville Island for Officers Quarters, agreeable to a plan and bill scantling to be seen at my office [Officer of the Agent for Prisoners of War]; the building to be completed by the 1st day of November next." For approval by the Transport Board to Warren, see ADM 98/286, p. 142, NA.

54. In their book on *Deadman's Island*, p. 61, Iris Shea and Heather Watts provide the following interpretation of the wording on the foundation stone:

> This Building
> Was Erected By Order Of Sir J.B.
> Warren Bt, K.B. Vice Admiral
> And Commander Of The North
> American Station And Under The
> Direction Of Capt. John Mckellar [sic]
> HM Navy
> Agent For The Prisoners Of War
> Who Laid The
> Foundation Stone The
> 1st Day Of Sep. A.D., 1808

Since its reported discovery in 1929 by Harry Piers of the Provincial Museum, it has been believed, incorrectly, to be the foundation stone for the prison barracks, which was built in 1805.

55. *Acadian Recorder* (Halifax), 4 September 1813.

56. Transport Office to Admiral Griffith, 6 May 1814, ADM 98/290, NA.

57. Allan Everett Marble, *Physicians, Pestilence, and the Poor: A History of Medicine and Social Conditions in Nova Scotia 1800-1867* (Victoria, B.C.: Trafford Publishing, 2000), p. 292, fn. 76.

58. Transport Board to Mitchell, 8 April 1806, ADM 98/286, pp. 19-20.

59. Transport Board to Captain Beresford, 3 July 1806, ADM 98/286, p. 60.

60. Transport Board to Vice Admiral G.C. Berkeley, 7 November 1806, ADM 98/286, NA.

61. Transport Board to MacKellar, 6 August 1807, ADM 98/286, NA.

62. Transport Board to Vice Admiral Sir J.B. Warren, 2 December 1807, ADM 98/286, NA.

63. Although Toler's plan of Melville Island shows a building opposite Deadman's Island marked as a hospital, the documentary evidence makes clear that the prison hospital was in the upper storey of the prison building. A possible explanation is that the building marked hospital had in the past served temporarily as a hospital.

CHAPTER 2

1. Robert Gardiner, *The Naval War of 1812* (Great Britain: Claxton Editions, 2001), p. 20.

2. *Ibid*. p. 19.

3. *Ibid*.

4. For a Nova Scotian perspective on the War of 1812, see John Boileau, *Halfhearted Enemies: Nova Scotia, New England and the War of 1812* (Halifax: Formac Publishing Company, 2005). The expression "a mere matter of marching" is attributed to Thomas Jefferson. Ronald J. Dale, *The Invasion of Canada: Battles of the War of 1812* (Toronto: James Lorimer & Company, 2001), p. 17.

5. As reported in the *New-Bedford Mercury* (New Bedford, MA), 3 January 1812, p. 2

6. As reported in the *New-England Palladium* (New York) 19 June 1812, p. 1.

7. For the most comprehensive list of prizes processed through the Court of Vice Admiralty in Halifax, see Faye Margaret Kert, *Prize and Prejudice: Privateering and Naval Prize in Atlantic Canada in the War of 1812* (St. John's, Newfoundland: Research in Maritime History, No. 11, International Maritime Economic History Association, 1997), pp. 159-203. For an analysis of the prizes captured, see also Wade G. Dudley, *Splintering the Wooden Wall: The British Blockade of the United States, 1812-1815* (Annapolis, Maryland: Naval Institute Press, 2003), p. 143.

8. *Boston Centinel* (Boston) 25 July 1812, as published in the *Columbian* (New York), 27 July 1812.

9. *Royal Gazette* (Halifax), 8 July 1812.

10. Margaret Faye Kert, *Prize and Prejudice*, p. 46.

11. *Salem Gazette* (Salem), 22 June 1812.

12. *Royal Gazette* (Halifax), 15 July 1812.

13. *Salem Gazette* (Salem), 30 October 1812.

14. Lieutenant William Miller to Lieutenant-Governor Sir James Kempt, 1 November 1822, MG100, vol. 189, no. 29, NSARM.

15. General Entry Book of American Prisoners of War Received by Lieutenant William Miller, Agent, Halifax, opened 25 June 1812, ADM 103/167, NA. It consists of 241 pages.

16. *New Hampshire Patriot* (Concord), 4 August 1812.

17. *New-York Spectator* (New York), 22 August 1812.

18. *Portsmouth Gazette* (Portsmouth), 17 August 1812.

19. *The Repertory & General Advertiser* (Boston), 28 July 1812.

20. *Boston Centinel* (Boston), 8 August 1812.

21. *Salem Gazette* (Salem), 18 August 1812.

22. Report in the *Salem Gazette* and printed in the *Portland Gazette*, 3 August 1812.

23. *Ibid*.

24. Vice Admiral Herbert Sawyer to William Croker, 17 September 1812, ADM 1/506, f. 266, NA.

25. *Columbian Centinel* (New York), 7 November 1812.

26. *American Watchman* (Wilmington), 31 October 1812.

27. *National Intelligencer* (Washington), 17 December 1812, taken from the *Baltimore American*, (Baltimore), 15 December 1812.

28. *Independent Chronicle* (Boston), 10 December 1812.

29. See notation in Entry Book, ADM103//167, NA, p. 130, "Received from Bermuda on order of the Commander-in-Chief supposed to be British subjects."

30. *The Naval War of 1812*, p. 47.

31. These figures are derived from the Entry Book, ADM103/167, NA.

32. *American Advocate*, (Hallowell, ME), 19 June 1813.

33. *Columbian* (New York), 7 June 1813.

34. *American Advocate* (Hallowell, ME), 19 June 1813.

35. *Yankee* (Boston), 9 July 1813.

36. Account of the Treatment of the Americans captured on board the privateer brig *Decatur* of Newburyport by Abel Coffin and

Richard O'Brien, Officers on board the privateer *Decatur*, Newburyport, August 2, 1813, *Essex Register* (Salem), 4 August 1813.

37. "Statement, Georgetown, December 29, 1813" published in the Federal Republican (Georgetown, Washington, D.C.), 29 December 1813 (hereafter "Statement")

38. Roger Masters, *Bold Privateers: Terror, Plunder and Profit on Canada's Atlantic Coast* (Halifax: Formac Publishing, 2004), pp. 115-16.

39. John Boileau, *Half-Hearted Enemies*, p. 68.

40. Sawyer to Croker, 20 August 1812, ADM 1/506, ff. 197-99, NA.

41. Sawyer to Croker, 17 September 1812, ADM 1/506, f. 266, NA.

42. Sawyer to Croker, acknowledging orders, ADM 1/506, f. 282, NA.

43. Lieutenant William Crane to Secretary of the Navy, 31 July 1813, RG 45, BC. 1812, vol. 2, no. 122, ALS, DNA, printed in William S. Dudley, *The Naval War of 1812, A Documentary History, vol. 1, 1812* (Washington, D.C.: Naval Historical Center, Department of the Navy, 2005), pp. 211-12 (hereafter *The Naval War of 1812: A Documentary History*).

44. The standard reference for the handling of prisoners of war during the War of 1812 in the United States remains Anthony Deitz, "The Prisoner of War in the United States during the War of 1812" (unpublished PhD thesis, The American University, 1964), (hereafter Deitz, "The Prisoner of War"). Copies can be obtained from University Microfilms, Inc., Ann Arbor, Michigan (no. 64-12, 801).

45. Secretary of State James Monroe to St. J. Baker, 28 August 1812, Papers of John Mitchell, vol. 1, pp. 52-53, Library of Congress (hereafter, Mitchell Papers).

46. Monroe to Mitchell, 7 September 1812, Mitchell Papers, vol. 1, pp. 56-57.

47. Mitchell to P. Hamilton, 7 October 1812, as quoted in Deitz, "The Prisoner of War," p. 25.

48. *Ibid.*, p. 26.

49. Earl Bathurst to Sir George Prevost, 18 November 1812, printed in *Select British Documents of the Canadian War of 1812*," vol. 3, part 2, Publications of the Champlain Society (1928), pp. 854-55.

50. Mitchell to P. Hamilton, 20 November 1812, as quoted in Deitz, "The Prisoner of War," p. 29

51. Mitchell to P. Hamilton, 20 November 1812, as quoted in Deitz, "The Prisoner of War," p. 30.

52. In ADM 1/503, f. 76, National Archives, London is a printed copy of *A PROVISIONAL AGREEMENT, for the Exchange of Naval Prisoners of War, made and concluded at HALIFAX, in the PROVINCE OF NOVA SCOTIA, on the 28th day of November in the year of our Lord One Thousand Eight Hundred and Twelve, between the Government of GREAT BRITAIN and the Government of the UNITED STATES OF AMERICA.* In Dietz, "The Prisoner of War" there is a photocopy of the document. The Avalon Project of Yale University Law School has put a version online. A copy of the Articles of Agreement arrived at the Admiralty in March 1813. See Minutes, Transport Board, Prisoners of War, 4 March 1813, ADM 99/230, NA.

53. Mitchell to P. Hamilton, 1 December 1812, quoted in Deitz, "The Prisoner of War," p. 34.

54. Thomas Barclay to Transport Board, 15 April 1813, printed in George Lockhart, *Selections from the Correspondence of Thomas Barclay* (New York, 1894), p. 326.

55. Transport Board to Barclay, 6 November 1813, in *ibid.*, p. 340.

56. Warren to Mitchell, 14 October 1812, John Mitchell Papers, vol. 1, p. 97.

57. Circular, Mitchell to Marshals, 13 February 1813, Mitchell Papers, vol. 2, p. 206.

58. Mitchell to Monroe, 16 April 1813, Mitchell Papers, vol. 2, pp. 242-44.

59. Jonathan Bruce and two others to Mitchell, 4 May 1813, Mitchell Papers, vol. 2, p. 255.

60. Miller to Mitchell, 16 August 1813, vol. 426, folder 1, John Mitchell Papers, Historical Society of Pennsylvania, Philadelphia.

61. Sherbrooke to Lord Bathurst, 1 September 1813, CO217/91, ff. 193-94, NA, and Bathurst to Sherbrooke, 8 October 1813, RG1, vol. 62, doc. 84, NSARM.

62. One such successful deception is well described in *Journal of A Young Man of Massachusetts late a Surgeon on Board An American Privateer…* (2nd. edition, 1816), pp. 25-26. (Hereafter *Journal of A Young Man of Massachusetts.*) The authorship of this journal has been attributed to a Benjamin Waterhouse, but recent research by Iris Shea and Heather Watts suggests that Waterhouse could not have been the "young man of Massachusetts" and that he collected his information from various individuals. For bibliographical information on the authorship, see *Deadman's*, endnote 31, pp. 104-05. However, in the text I have used the name of Benjamin Waterhouse as the person whose experiences are recorded in the journal because that attribution appears in nearly all publications referring to the journal. Also, stylistically the journal is clearly by one hand, whatever the sources of information.

63. Mitchell to Miller, 4 October 1813, John Mitchell Papers, vol. 3, p. 404.

64. Mason to Mitchell, 8 November 1813, Mitchell Papers, vol. 3, p. 426-27.

65. Sherbrooke to Bathurst, 16 December 1813, RG1, vol. 62, doc. 109, NSARM.

66. Mitchell to Rueben Beazley, 16 August 1814, Mitchell Papers, vol. 4, p. 632.

67. Mason to Mitchell, 17 August 1814, Mitchell Papers, vol. 4, p. 633.

68. Mitchell to Beazley, 23 August 1814, Mitchell Papers, vol. 4, p. 639.

69. Mitchell to Monroe, 22 September 1814, Mitchell Papers, vol. 4, p. 646.

70. Mitchell to James Prince, 11 October 1814, Mitchell Papers, vol. 4, p. 647.

71. H.F. Pullen, *The Shannon and the Chesapeake* (Toronto: McClelland & Stewart, 1970), pp. 60-61.

72. Extract of a letter from Dr. Swift to a friend in Boston, 8 June 1813, printed in the *Portland Gazette*, 28 June 1813.

73. H.F. Pullen, *The Shannon and the Chesapeake*, Appendix F: Muster roll of the officers and men belonging to the late United States frigate *Chesapeake*, who were carried to Halifax as prisoners of war, pp. 147-154.

74. As reported in the *Salem Gazette* (Salem), 10 August 1813.

75. *American Advocate* (Hallowell, ME), 14 August 1813.

76. *Ibid.*, 28 August 1813.

77. See comment by "Enemies," entitled "Friends of the Navy, 'By their works ye shall know them,'" *Essex Register* (Salem), 12 March 1814. The piece was written relating to a motion in the American Senate "that it is improper for a moral and religious people to do honor to deeds of glory done in this unholy and parricidal [*sic*] war against our parent state…."

78. *Portland Gazette*, (Portland), 8 August 1814.

CHAPTER 3

1. The title for this chapter comes from *The Diary of Benjamin F. Palmer, Privateersman: While a prisoner on board English warships, in the prison at Melville Island and at Dartmoor* (New Haven: The Tuttle, Morehouse & Taylor Press, The Acorn Series, 1914, No. 11). The verse appears on p. 266. (Hereafter *Diary of Benjamin F. Palmer.*)

2. "A Poem Composed by A Prisoner on Melville Island," printed in the *Diary of Benjamin F. Palmer*, p. 228.

3. *Journal of A Young Man of Massachusetts*, p. 18.

4. For a genealogical note on William Sutherland, see Iris Shea and Heather Watts, *Deadman's*, p. 35.

5. *Ned Myers, or A Life Before the Mast* (English edition, c. 1843), p. 93. Myers says that "It was said the people of the canteens had about four hundred of the dollars, when they came to overhaul their lockers." *Weekly Chronicle* (Halifax), 4 February 1814 for notice. Myers,

another captured privateersman, told his life story to James Fenimore Cooper, who published it. Myers grew up in Halifax before running away to sea at age eleven (pp. 91-107). After he was freed from Melville Prison at the peace, he was reunited briefly with his sister, who had married and remained in Halifax.

6. *Ned Myers, or A Life Before the Mast*, p. 93. "Quino" is Spanish for a game called Keno, which resembles bingo and is based on the drawing of numbers and the covering of corresponding numbers on cards. It was apparently very popular among seamen. I am indebted to Francis I.W. Jones for this information.

7. *Diary of Benjamin F. Palmer*, p. 57.

8. *Journal of A Young Man of Massachusetts*, p. 14.

9. *Diary of Benjamin F. Palmer*, p. 79.

10. *Journal of a Young Man of Massachusetts*, p. 17.

11. *Ibid.*, p. 57.

12. Regulations established by the Committee appointed by the Magority [sic] of the Prisoners, dated 11 October 1814, Benjamin F. Palmer, Secretary, printed in the *Diary of Benjamin F. Palmer*, pp. 244-46. It is possible that Palmer brought this set of regulations with him from Melville Prison.

13. *Ibid.*, p. 244.

14. *Ibid.* p. 232.

15. For a list of American Prisoners of War who escaped, see *Deadman's*, appendix VIII, pp. 89-90.

16. Mason to Mitchell, 4 June 1814, Mitchell Papers, vol. 3, pp. 566-67.

17. Mitchell to Mason, undated, but June? 1813, Mitchell Papers, vol. 3, p. 488.

18. Thomas Swain to Mitchell, undated, but 1813, Mitchell Papers, vol. 3, p. 505.

19. *Weekly Chronicle* (Halifax), 12 November 1813.

20. John Mitchell to John Mason, 29 August 1814, Mitchell Papers, vol. 4, p. 643. Mitchell believed eleven had escaped, though the Entry Book has the number at nine.

21. His claim to three successful escapes was made at Salem and published in the *Columbian* (New York), 10 September 1814.

22. Dates can be found in the General Entry Book, ADM103/167. See also *Deadman's*, p. 90.

23. *Ned Myers, or A Life Before the Mast*, p. 105. Interestingly, in the summer of 1814 prisoners at Dartmoor used the tunnel idea, but as at Melville Island an informer gave them away.

24. Mitchell to Monroe, 23 January 1813, vol. 1, p. 192.

25. Anthony Dietz, "The Prisoner of War," p. 166. Instructions were dated 17 August 1813.

26. Mitchell to Monroe, 23 January 1813, Mitchell Papers, vol. 1, p. 189.

27. Miller to Mitchell, 4 December 1813, vol. 426, folder 1, John Mitchell Papers, Historical Society of Pennsylvania, Philadelphia.

28. Joseph Livery to Mitchell, Melville Island, 17 July 1813, Mitchell Papers, vol. 2, p. 312.

29. Miller to Mitchell, 29 November 1813, Mitchell Papers, vol. 3, p. 460.

30. "A Poem Composed by A Prisoner on Melville Island," printed in the *Diary of Benjamin F. Palmer*, p. 236.

31. Excerpt of a letter in the *Mercantile Advertiser* (New York), 3 November 1813, printed in "The War," vol. 2, 21 December 1813, p. 110.

32. *Ibid.*

33. *Ibid.*

34. John Mitchell's Petition to the Senate and House of Representatives, 12 January 1824, Mitchell Papers.

35. Mason to Mitchell, 8 November 1813, vol. 3, and William Prince, Marshall, District of Massachusetts, to John Mitchell, 20 November 1813, vol. 426, folder 1, John Mitchell Papers, Historical Society of Pennsylvania, Philadelphia.

36. Receipt for payment of 314 shoes and 224 stockings for American Prisoners of War by William Miller to John Mitchell, 4 January 1814, vol. 3, p. 551. There are lists in the Mitchell papers prepared by prison officials, c. 1814, giving the prisoner's name and items of clothing — hats, shoes, jackets, trousers, shirts, vests and shoes — issued to each individual. Shoes were the most frequent item, 939 pairs being issued. The Transport Board approved of Miller's action in providing clothing and ordered him to receive in value from Mitchell of the items supplied to American prisoners. See Transport Board to Miller, 7 April 1814, ADM 98/290, NA.

37. *Diary of Benjamin E. Palmer*, p. 59.

38. Miller to Mitchell, 29 November 1813, vol. 3, p. 459. 180.

39. The letter was dated Melville Island Prison, Jan. 9, 1814 and appeared in the *Newburyport Herald* (Newburyport, MA), 4 February 1814.

40. Officers in Prison to John Mitchell, 15 June 1814, Mitchell Papers, vol. 4, p. 598

41. Printed in *The Diary of Benjamin F. Palmer*, p. 242.

42. Reginald Horsman, "The Paradox of Dartmoor Prison," *American Heritage Magazine*, 20 (1975), p. 15.

43. Mitchell to Marshall of the United States District of Boston, 21 November 1812, Mitchell Papers, vol. 1, p 126.

44. *Ibid.*

45. Mitchell to Secretary of the Navy, 1 March 1813, Mitchell Papers, vol. 2, p. 214. At the time Mitchell was reporting to the Secretary of the Navy. See Paul Springer, "American Prisoner of War Policy," p. 64-65 on the policy relating to blacks.

46. Mitchell to Mr. Prince, marshal in Boston, 22 December 1812, Mitchell Papers, vol. 1, pp. 153-54.

47. Mitchell to John H. Barnes, 2 February 1813, Mitchell Papers, vol. 2, p. 198.

48. Mitchell to H. Dearborn, 30 May 1813, Mitchell Papers, vol. 2, p. 275.

49. Mitchell to Mason, 14 August 1813, Mitchell Papers, vol. 2, pp. 357-58.

50. See "Supplying the Enemy by a gentleman from Halifax, late a prisoner there ...," *Columbian* (New York), 3 August 1813.

51. *American Advocate* (Hallowell, ME), 20 November 1813.

52. *Ibid.*

53. See for example under the title "Smuggling Trade & Traitor's Rights." An enraged reader wrote "Give us information, by our spurious neutrals, give support to 200 American traitors residing at Halifax...." *American Advocate* (Hallowell, ME), 27 November 1813.

54. *Ibid.*, 1 January 1814.

55. *New Hampshire Patriot* (Concord), 1 February 1814.

56. Sherbrooke to Warren, 16 December 1813, RG1, vol. 62, doc. 62, NSARM.

57. *Diary of Benjamin F. Palmer*, p. 53.

58. *Journal of A Young Man of Massachusetts*, p. 15.

59. *Diary of Benjamin F. Palmer*, pp. 66-67.

60. For example, see Alexander M. Anderson to John Mitchell, 25 November 1813, Mitchell Papers, vol. 3, p. 442. Anderson, who was on parole in Dartmouth, reported that Miller's language to him "was such as no man would bear without resenting had he the opportunity."

61. Miller to Mitchell, 29 November 1813, Mitchell Papers, vol. 3, pp. 454-59.

62. In his letter Miller said that charges of cruelty were published in a Portland paper of 21 September 1813. However, a search of the Maine papers — the *Portland Gazette*, *Eastern Argus* and *American Advocate* — found no such references. As will be discussed below any such charges did not appear until November issues.

63. *Journal of a Young Man of Massachusetts*, p. 16.

64. *Ibid.*
65. *Eastern Argus* (Portland), 11 November 1813.
66. General Entry Book of all the Prisoners of War sent to the Hospital at Melville Island between 6 October 1813 and 31 March 1815, ADM 103/241.
67. *Eastern Argus*, (Portland), 18 November 1813.
68. *Portland Gazette* (Portland), 15 November 1813.
69. *Portland Gazette* (Portland), 26 March 1814. The letter was dated 3 March 1814, Melville Island Depot. The same letter appeared in the *Acadian Recorder*, 19 March 1814.
70. *Essex Register* (Salem), 13 August 1814.
71. *Ibid.*
72. *New York Gazette and Weekly Advertiser* (New York), 14 December 1814.
73. *Boston Gazette* (Boston), 29 April 1814.
74. *Acadian Recorder* (Halifax), 17 February 1814.

CHAPTER 4

1. For what follows, see "Statement."
2. Donald R. Hickey, *The War of 1812: A Forgotten Conflict*, p. 177-78. Paul Springer has the prisoners taken at the Battle of Queenston Heights placed on boats to Halifax. However, the Melville Island prisoner Entry Book has no American soldiers arriving until June 1813.
3. Deitz, "The Prisoner of War," p. 248.
4. "Statement". When the British naval authorities could not find sufficient evidence to convict the six, they sent them to Charleston where the Americans released the 12 British prisoners. It is uncertain whether the full details of this transaction were known in Halifax.
5. Mitchell to Miller, 3 September 1813, Mitchell Papers, vol. 3, p. 369.
6. Mason to John Mitchell, 13 November 1813, Mitchell Papers, vol. 3, pp. 433. After receiving Mitchell's report, Mason had sent it to President Madison who ordered him to place a corresponding number and grade of British prisoners under "a rigor of treatment, corresponding with that authenticated to be used against American prisoners." Madison considered that the sending of prisoners, particularly privateers, to England could not be justified by any "plea of necessity or safety." Madison to Mason, 23 September 1813, ALS, MiU-C, War of 1812, printed in William S. Dudley, *The Naval War of 1812, A Documentary History, Vol. II, 1813* (Washington, D.C.: Naval Historical Center, Department of the Navy, 2005), pp. 248-49.
7. "Statement".
8. *Ibid.*
9. Printed in the *Portland Gazette* (Portland), 18 October 1813.
10. *Eastern Argus* (Portland), 23 September 1813.
11. *Ibid.*
12. *Portland Gazette* (Portland), 18 September 1813.
13. *Eastern Argus* (Portland), 30 September 1813, and *Portland Gazette* (Portland), 28 September 1813.
14. An unsigned communication to the *Acadian Recorder* (Halifax), 11 December 1813.
15. Miller to Mitchell, September 1813, vol. 3, pp. 579-81.
16. *American Advocate*, 1 January 1814.
17. John Mason to John Mitchell, 7 June 1814, Mitchell Papers, vol. 3, pp. 422-24.
18. *Ibid.*
19. Paul Springer, "American Prisoner of War Policy," p. 80.
20. George Lockhart Rivers, *Selections from the Correspondence of Thomas Barclay*, pp. 317-18.
21. *Ibid.*
22. Mason to Mitchell, 6 November 1813, Mitchell Papers, vol. 3, pp. 422-24.
23. Quoted in *Deadman's Island*, p. 32.
24. Admiral Edward Griffith to Captain Cochet, 13 November 1814, and Cochet to Mitchell, 14 November 1814, Mitchell Papers, vol. 4, p. 678.
25. *Acadian Recorder*, 26 November 1814.
26. John Mitchell's Petition to the Senate and House of Representatives, 12 January 1824. Mitchell Papers.
27. Petition of John Osborn to Sherbrooke, asking for letters of marque and reprisal, 2 September 1813, RG1, vol. 227, doc. 31.
28. Reports from New York, 14 and 15 December, of the arrival of the British cartel *Jane and Martha Ridout* from Halifax, printed in the *Eastern Argus*, 22 December 1814.
29. Mason to Mitchell, 17 August 1814, Mitchell Papers, vol. 4, p. 534.
30. *Acadian Recorder* (Halifax), 26 November 1814.
31. Transport Board to Miller, 26 November 1813, ADM 98/290, NA.
32. *Diary of Benjamin F. Palmer*, 9 June 1814, p. 73.
33. Transport Board to Miller, 6 November 1813, ADM 98/290, NA.
34. See issues of the *Acadian Recorder* (Halifax), 30 July, 6 August, 13 August and 27 August 1814. Dianne Marshall in "Halifax caught in two World Wars," Novascotian section, Halifax *Sunday Herald* 4 September 2005, pp. 3-4, says that Miller was guilty of corruption. Sir John Sherbrooke seems not to have believed so, as he wrote Miller on hearing that the agent had to relinquish his appointment at Halifax, that he would "at all times be happy to bear the most ample testimony to your worth." Sherbrooke to Miller, 10 May 1814, a copy with William Miller to Lieutenant-Governor Sir James Kempt, 1 November 1822, MG100, vol. 189, no. 29, NSARM.
35. *Acadian Recorder* (Halifax), 27 August 1814.
36. Sherbrooke to Miller, 10 May 1814, a copy with William Miller to Lieutenant-Governor Sir James Kempt, 1 November 1822, MG100, vol. 189, no. 38, NSARM.
37. For Miller's marriage to Sarah Tucker, see *Deadman's*, p. 31. F.W. Bowes, writing in the *Acadian Recorder* (Halifax), 16 January 1913, says that Miller's wife (unnamed) was the aunt of the father of the present editor of the *Acadian Recorder*, Charles Blackadar).
38. *Salem Gazette* (Salem), 19 August 1814.
39. The *American Advocate* (Hallowell, ME), 25 February 1815 printed the treaty as ratified by the two nations.
40. Transport Board to Commissioner P. Wodehouse, 22 March 1815, HAL/E/3b, Halifax Dockyard Records, Commissioners Records, NA.
41. *Ned Myers, or A Life before the Mast*, pp. 106-07.
42. *American Advocate*, (Hallowell, ME) 1 April 1815.
43. General Entry Book of all the Prisoners of War sent to the Hospital at Melville Island between 6 October 1813 and 31 March 1815, ADM 103/241.
44. Mitchell to Mason, 22 September 1814, Mitchell Papers, vol. 4, pp. 646-47.
45. *American Advocate*, 22 April 1815.
46. As quoted in Reginald Horsman, "The Paradox of Dartmoor Prison", p. 85
47. Transport Office to Commissioner Philip Wodehouse, 3 November 1815, HAL/E/3b, Halifax Dockyard Records, Commissioners Records, NA.
48. *Nova-Scotia Royal Gazette*, 19 December 1815. Miller as resident agent placed an advertisement for seamen to crew the *Mentor* transport.
49. Wodehouse to Transport Board 1 February 1816, HAL/E/3b, Halifax Dockyard Records, Commissioners Records, NA.
50. *Acadian Recorder* (Halifax), 17 February 1817.
51. Transport Board Minutes, 7 August 1816, ADM, 98/290, NA.
52. William Miller versus Thomas Haigh Mason, deposition sworn by Miller, 8 August 1814, Nova Scotia Supreme Court, RG 39, series C, vol. 104, NSARM. Miller signed the deposition, and his signature

matches his signature found in the Mitchell Papers.

53. Miller to Kempt, 1 November 1822, MG100, vol. 189, no. 29, NSARM. Miller's reason for writing Kempt was to avoid having a grant of land escheated because no improvements had been made. Miller said that he had a large family and intended the land for his sons. In the letter he stated that he had returned to England in 1816. In 1822 he was living on the island of Jersey.
54. Miller to Kempt, 1 November 1822, MG100, vol. 189, no. 29, NSARM.
55. *Diary of Benjamin F. Palmer*, pp. 68-69 and 72.
56. "A Poem Composed by A Prisoner on Melville Island," printed in the *Diary of Benjamin F. Palmer*, pp. 232-33.
57. Naval Hospital Records are found in ADM 102/260-264, NA, for the years 1803-15, and there are copies in the Maritime Command Museum, Halifax. I am grateful to Dr. Allan E. Marble for bringing this collection to my attention.
58. Account of French Prisoners of War who have Died at Halifax, and similarly for Spaniards, ADM103/625, NA. For a list of French prisoners of war who died at Halifax, 1803-1813, see *Deadman's*, Appendix III, pp. 73-74.
59. List of Sick and Wounded Seamen and Soldiers American Prisoners of War, ADM103/625, NA Calculation of Iris Shea of the Halifax Mainland South Heritage Society.

CHAPTER 5

1. Deitz, "Prisoners of War," p. 134.
2. Benjamin Waterhouse, Journal of a Young Man of Massachusetts, p. 33.

EPILOGUE

1. John N. Grant, *The Immigration & Settlement of the Black Refugees of the War of 1812 in Nova Scotia and New Brunswick* (Dartmouth, N.S., Black Cultural Centre, 1990), p. 67
2. Thomas Chandler Haliburton, *An Historical and Statistical Account of Nova Scotia*, vol. 2, pp. 22-23.
3. Susan Morse, "Immigration to Nova Scotia, 1839-1851" (M.A. the-sis, Dalhousie University, April 1946), p. 90. For the most comprehensive description of the Quarantine Hospital (1818-47), see Iris Shea and Heather Watts, *Deadman's*, pp. 38-39.
4. Report of the Special Committee, *Journal and Proceedings of the House of Assembly*, 1848, Appendix 62.
5. Provincial Secretary's Papers, RG7, no. NSARM.
6. Iris Shea and Heather Watts, *Deadman's*, p. 41.
7. For a summary of the negotiations and history of Melville Island as a military prison, see Major H. Meredith Logan, "Melville Island, The Military Prison of Halifax," pp. 22-23.
8. John Boileau gives a date of 1884 in "A very humble garrison," in the Novascotian section of the Halifax *Sunday Herald*, 29 May 2005. Boileau relied on J.P. LeBlanc, who had 1884 as the date in his History of the Armdale Yacht Club. However, Harry Piers in *The Evolution of the Halifax Fortress 1749-1928* (Halifax: Public Archives of Nova Scotia, 1947), p. 62 has the date of 1905 for construction of "a block of new stone cells, well lighted, ventilated, and heated" which were "an addition to the long, pitched-roof building, erected in 1809 to accommodate French prisoners-of-war, which still stands [1928]." Iris Shea and Heather Watts (in *Deadman's*, endnote no. 7, p. 106) were not able to find confirmation of either date.
9. John W. Regan, *Sketches and Traditions of the Northwest Arm* (first printing, 1908), p. 117.
10. For Longley and Deadman's Island, see Iris Shea and Heather Watts, *Deadman's*, p. 62
11. John Regan, *Sketches and Traditions of the Northwest Arm*, pp. 110-12.
12. Scott Robson, Nova Scotia Museum, located a note made by Harry Piers to this effect.
13. For the story of these internees, see Iris Shea and Heather Watts, *Deadman's*, pp. 51-55. Appendix XI lists the names of those interned, pp. 96-100.
14. For the history of Armdale Yacht Club, see J.P. LeBlanc, A Detailed History of the Armdale Yacht Club (armdaleyachtclub.ns.ca) and Iris Shea and Heather Watts, *Deadman's*, pp. 59-61
15. For the story of the efforts by community groups to ensure the preservation of Deadman's Island, see Iris Shea and Heather Watts, *Deadman's* pp. 62-67.

PHOTO CREDITS

INDEX